THE INDIAN ROOTS
OF VACCINATION

Mitra Desai

INDIA • SINGAPORE • MALAYSIA

Website: www.mitradesai.com

Cover design: Horia Sidiqi

CONTENTS

Contents

FOREWORD

It is easier to trace the contours of medical history when you know what to look for. Or whom. Therein lies a peculiar pattern in our scientific chronicles - a gallery of Western names immortalised while their Indian predecessors remain shrouded in deliberate anonymity.

There is something about this selective remembering that Mitra Desai's "Śītalā" confronts with remarkable precision. The colonial record-keeping being what it is — systematically hierarchical, a disturbing asymmetry emerges. Who gets named and who remains nameless? Who becomes history and who becomes folklore? Who is a scientist and who is merely a 'native practitioner'? Many a Western practitioners are catalogued with meticulous detail - their birthplaces, their methods, their patients, their personal lives - while the Indian practitioners dissolve into the mists of collective nouns: 'Tikadars', 'Brahmins', 'native inoculators'.

The art of historical erasure works not just through denial but through deliberate anonymization. Through her masterful storytelling, Mitra breathes life into a story that has been neglected so far. Indeed, while we know James Phipps was the eight-year-old boy Dr Edward Jenner first vaccinated, or of Lady Montagu's children who received the variolation, yet we know nothing of the variolators whose cure kept these children alive.

These unnamed practitioners, working for nothing more than just 'cowries', carried on practice that predated Western medicine by centuries. Their methods, documented by bewildered colonial observers, revealed not just technical skill but a profound grasp of what we now call public health. This is the story Mitra tells - not through dry academic prose, but through the engaging device of intergenerational dialogue between a sceptical modern protagonist and her history-keeper grandfather.

What Mitra achieves here is nothing short of extraordinary. Through her narrative prowess, she unravels a story where history, science, and cultural memory converge to illuminate an inescapable realisation - that modern vaccination stands upon the foundations of Indian knowledge. This revelation, much like her protagonist's own journey from disbelief to understanding, forces us to confront not just what we know about medical history, but how we came to know it.

As a scientist who has witnessed firsthand the systematic erasure of Indian contributions from mainstream discourse, I find this work particularly significant. It does what generations of academic papers could not - it makes India's role in medicine impossible to ignore. Through her narrative technique that transforms complex medical history into an engaging family drama, Mitra makes this crucial story accessible to readers of all ages.

This is more than a historical correction. It is a restoration of dignity to a knowledge system that enabled one of humanity's greatest achievements, only to be written out of its own story. A story that finally gives voice to those unnamed practitioners - the true pioneers - and draws them out of the shadows of anonymity into the light of recognition they so richly deserve.

This book isn't just meant to be read; it is meant to be shared, discussed, and used as a template for reclaiming countless other erased chapters of Indian scientific achievement. The time for quiet acceptance of historical distortion is over. The time for reclaiming our narrative has begun.

– Dr. Anand Ranganathan

Scientist and Author: The Land of the Wilted Rose (Rupa). Love & Honour; The Rat Eater (Bloomsbury). Soufflé (Penguin).

PRAISE FOR ŚĪTALĀ

Mitra's Śītalā is a journey of Asatoma Sadgamay- a journey from untruth, lies, and narratives to the Truth. This is the journey of decolonization beyond India, that is, Bharat. A compelling journey through Tara, as painful and insightful for the reader as it was for the central character of Tara. Storytelling is an art. Decolonization of narratives is a science. Mitra Desai beautifully combines both the art and science in Śītalā. The war of narratives and making people aware of their colonized myopic understanding of one's own culture and civilization has reached a new height where having our rootedness and voice are very critical. Pandemic times have proved how the world needs to wake up to Healthcare as Swasthya, and not just sickness care. Ayurveda has been far ahead than the rest of the medical systems in the world. Ayurveda is a science, not just a tradition. Hence, smallpox was known as Basant roga. Ayurveda knew the interconnectedness of seasons and human beings.

Śītalā works at many levels. One, of course, it questions the myth of modern medicine and reestablishing Ayurveda as a science. Two, how diseases are used as weapons by colonizers to not just wipe out people, but the knowledge held by the elders in these communities across the globe. Mitra Desai deserves applause for combining wisdom and science, storytelling, and insightful revelations, balancing pain of colonization and joy of becoming decolonized.

Prof. Mala Kapadia, Principle Investigator for Project Wellbeing and Happiness based on Ayurveda.

***

If you want to educate the masses; do it through storytelling. Mitra Desai's 'Śītalā' is an ideal example of this. The author narrates a story backed up with historical references, ample footnotes and bibliography. Āyurveda is a well-developed life science which has been deliberately neglected over decades. The book is an eye-opener for the same. It narrates Āyurvedic references of Śītalā, Masūrikā and contemporary references of their Bhāratīya treatment in a refreshing manner. Although it is a lesser known fact; *Ayurvediya Suchividnyanam* (Āyurvedic Vaccination) has references from texts like *Sharangdhar Samhitā*. It was a profound practice in ancient Bhārat. The author has made an extraordinary effort to show this historical fact the light of day. I congratulate her and thank her as well on behalf of the entire Ayurvediya Vaidya fraternity.

Vaidya Dr. Pareexit Shevde; MD (Ayu.) Author of Streeyanche arogya ani Ayurved and Jamat -e-purogami.

***

I felt it was such a great idea and a wonderful way to narrate our numerous Bhāratīya nuggets that we are all so woefully unaware of! That these stories need to be told, need to be shared widely, need to be chronicled by us, the Bhāratīya people. So much technical information and historical accounts were researched and put together. We have always known (blurred and vague though) of the deep Bhāratīya gold mine we sprung from but to see it unfold with such clarity is a wonderful experience. What an effort Mitra, Congratulations!

Dr. Lakshmi Saripalli; Scientist and Radio Astronomer

***

Mitra Desai's timely work unveils an ignored aspect of India's indigenous medical wisdom. This book shines a light on sophisticated vaccination protocols our ancestors possessed - meticulously planning preventive healthcare with precise seasonal strategies and detailed dietary guidelines long before the West. We have tragically forgotten our civilizational brilliance, becoming like leaves disconnected from a magnificent tree. This systemic amnesia renders us vulnerable as it allows the erasure of our rich scientific and cultural heritage. Heartiest congratulations to Mitra.

Sahana Singh; Columnist, Editor, Speaker and Author of popular books The Educational Heritage of Ancient India – How an Ecosystem of Learning was Laid to Waste and Revisiting the Educational Heritage of India.

***

Reading this book, a deeply emotional experience for me. It struck a chord with me on two separate but interconnected levels. Over 50 years ago my school education was in an Indian Public School, modeled on British schools of the type one might have read about in books by Enid Blyton. I was taught to view Indians with derision, as worthless, lazy people needing improvement. Indians were accused of being ahistorical, with their itihasas and puranas being fairy tales.

In my all-boys school, mischievous students were punished using terms reserved for Indians such as "chokra boy" or worse "ruddy Tatiya", where Tatiya was a contemptuous reference to freedom fighter Tantia Tope, who was an undesirable in the eyes of the ethos of my school Later when I studied medicine and went on to become a surgeon, I was taught to be derisive of Indian systems and Indian forms of medicine. I had to learn about diseases as viewed from the West.

As I grew older and wiser, putting many decades of practice under my belt. I realized how unfair my education had been, Indians were not stupid or lazy and over the years I underwent a deep decolonization of my mind. Along with that I learned about ancient Indian health practices that were simply ignored or unrecognized, including Suśruta's surgical techniques, hand cleaning and no-touch techniques used in ancient India that were exactly what surgeons do in operating theaters, and simple acts like boiling milk for sterilization.

This book is a beautifully constructed story of the decolonization of the mind of a young lady named Tārā who is the protagonist of the book. Tārā's education and attitudes were exactly like mine, deracinated, contemptuous of all things Indian and admiring of anything from the West. The story shows the gradual awareness that Tārā gains about the past of her own people which echo my own experiences. Perhaps the most significant part is that the story is written like our puranas, It is not written as a textbook, or a bland history book.

Mitra Desai combines ineluctable historic facts cocooned inside the story of a family that could be almost any Indian family. It is woven around a delightful story in exactly the same way that our own Indian epics and narratives inform us of our past via the medium of enchanting stories. Thank you for writing this Mitra Desai. I recommend this book to all Indians. You will not regret reading it.

Dr Shiv Sastry; Surgeon and Author of critically acclaimed books Aryan Invasion: Myth or Fact? Uncovering the evidence and Pakistan Failed State & its Effect on India.

***

Successful and long-lasting civilizations have many common features: innovation, improvisation, ingenuity, endurance in action, freedom of thought, a conviction in absolute moral values, and philosophical foundations that enable problem-solving. This list of ingredients is not a secret. However, laziness and carelessness can enter anytime, and while such wisdom may not be in short supply, it may be "more honored in the breach than the observance." The fall or degradation of civilization is not far behind.

Civilizations maintain and improve their vibrancy through grand narratives, yet those built on factoids cannot last. Ancient epics like Ramayana and Mahabharata contain allusions to culture, philosophy, medicine, science, and technology, and their insights were conveyed by parents and grandparents to the next generation.

This effective transmission of grand narratives has been hampered by the deracination of 5+ generations of Indians, leading to ignorance of Indian civilization's original contributions, its grandeur, and its continuing insights for innovations, sustainable living, and solutions to some of the toughest problems in health, science, and technology.

It takes a village to raise a child. Multiple approaches to educating and enlightening the masses, in an entertaining fashion, are required for the effective transmission of ancient science and wisdom to current generations. I felt the current genres were not enough or adequate. I expressed this frustration to Mitra. This book is her response, and it has over-delivered against my expectations. She has created a new genre in history writing!

Śītalā's message is multifold, and I want readers to discover it on their own, suitable for their situation. Mitra has taken up a complex subject, peeled back all but the critical core, and has set out the fundamental truths of Dharma in a simple, understandable, and enjoyable form.

Śītalā is a fascinating yet fun read, but the message is dead serious. I wholeheartedly recommend this book as desired reading for children, young adults, business professionals, parents and grandparents, academics, entrepreneurs, and corporate bigwigs. Śītalā inspires all to be pragmatic and creative, to experiment in their specific fields, to improvise, and to solve hard problems. It serves as a guidepost to be creative, self-confident, and self-sufficient. Let grandparents read it to their grandchildren and children read it to their parents.

Nilesh Nilkanth Oak - Original researcher, TEDx speaker and Author of the best selling "Rama Ravana Yudh - 12209 BCE" and "When did the Mahabharata War Happen?

***

Dedication

This book is dedicated my Ajo, Appa ajoba and Nana.

Three brilliant and benevolent healers, who served selflessly.

These are the many conversations I wish I had with them.

Appa ajoba – Dr Narhar Sakharam Dudhgaonkar

Ajo – Dr Balkrushna Raghunath Kshirsagar

Nana – Dr Lakshman Vitthal Desai

And to all practitioners

who continue

to heal.

PREFACE

"You do not understand what your book has done for us," she said, her voice trembling with emotion. And until that encounter, I truly did not understand.

In a corner of the bustling Dharma in Digital Age conference at Atlanta, amid the academic buzz, this unexpected moment of profound connection unfolded quietly. The Indian-American mother's hands were wrapped tightly around mine, her grip conveying emotions that words alone could not express. Here we were, two mothers living in different continents united by shared heritage and the power of storytelling.

This was not just a reader thanking an author; it was a recognition of how crucial it is for our next generations to see their heritage reflected in stories of global significance. This and several such moments of connection, with parents, elders and most importantly next generation or readers, were not just touching – they were transformative. It made me acutely aware of the responsibility I carried.

As this and several such moments in the conference hall subsided, I found myself drawn in a different setting - the David J Spencer CDC (Center for Disease Control) Museum, Atlanta. The exhibit on smallpox, with its poignant artifacts like Shapona, the Yoruba god of smallpox, and the Ped-O-Jet used in the campaign to eradicate this once-devastating disease and more. Here, amidst the historic photographs and medical instruments, was a small murti of Śītalā—The Hindu goddess of both the cause and cure of smallpox.

It was at that moment that I felt Śītalā was unfinished business. Some stories were left untold in the first book. My own understanding of the topic had evolved since the original writing. It was time to add the new information and update the knowledge base.

What began as an intention to add a few chapters evolved into something far more comprehensive. As I delved into updating the research, I found myself drawn deeper into the narrative. Soon, I was reimagining entire sections while staying true to the original storyline and characters. What emerged is essentially a new book that preserves the heart of the original but offers a richer, more nuanced telling of this crucial history. The familiar characters remain our guides, but they now lead us through previously unexplored territories of this remarkable story.

The devastating use of smallpox as a tool of colonisation against indigenous populations worldwide, the genius of the Tikar brahmins and their subsequent systematic erasure from mainstream medical history are important additions.

This book aims to help us understand that our ancestral knowledge was neither peripheral nor accidental – it was foundational and deliberate. More importantly, it connects our heritage to a larger global narrative of indigenous wisdom and resilience.

"Śītalā" now offers a more holistic picture of how India enabled vaccination, weaving together erased history, colonial politics, and cultural wisdom. This is my attempt to honor both the known and forgotten pioneers, ensuring that future generations inherit not just the triumph of vaccination but also get a glimpse of the complex human story behind it.

The introduction section of this book serves as a foundation for the academic discussion that forms its core. For those interested in purely the storytelling, the primary narrative begins in the first chapter. However, readers seeking deeper insight into the subject matter will find the introduction essential, as it lays out the historical and scientific context that underpins this exploration. Therefore, while you can skip ahead to the narrative, appreciating the scholarship that precedes it will enrich your understanding of the themes and arguments presented in the subsequent chapters.

To maintain the reader's momentum and readability, all references that have informed the story are strategically placed at the story's conclusion.

Whatever wisdom emerges in these pages—is solely by the divine grace of Śrī Rāma. My ancestors, whose wisdom flows through my veins, have guided this journey of discovery and understanding.

Any imperfections, limitations, or inadvertent errors that may have slipped into this work are entirely my own—a testament to human fallibility.

Offered at the lotus feet of Śrī Rāma.

INTRODUCTION

Long before Edward Jenner became the celebrated father of vaccination by finding a cure for smallpox, India had a sophisticated system of inoculation against smallpox. While Europe grappled with devastating epidemics, lacking fundamental understanding, Indian practitioners had mastered inoculation aka variolation—a safe and effective treatment method.

We are told that inoculation was primitive and perilous, whereas vaccination represents the pinnacle of scientific precision. Inoculation was a high-risk practice fraught with multiple vulnerabilities—direct exposure to live pathogens, unpredictable transmission risks, and uncontrolled immune responses. The primitive solution with high potential for widespread infection, rudimentary understanding of pathogen dynamics, inconsistent procedural standards, and practices deeply rooted in localized cultural contexts. Each intervention was a potential gamble with human life.

Vaccination, by contrast, emerged as a revolutionary approach. Meticulously engineered biological agents replaced dangerous live pathogens. Controlled pathogen introduction minimized infection risks, providing unprecedented ability to predict biological outcomes. Scientifically validated protocols and standardized manufacturing processes transformed medical intervention from a risky experiment to a precise, calculable protection mechanism.

The word "vaccine" derives from "vacca"—Latin for cow—we hear this ad nauseum. Today we have come to think of inoculation and vaccination as two different disciplines, but are they really? Or was it a masterclass in marketing and intellectual appropriation. Unquestioningly, we accept this evolutionary trajectory—from dangerous, haphazard practices to a scientifically calibrated, precisely controlled intervention and divine deliverance handed to us through Jenner. This book does not aim to diminish the contributions of Edward Jenner, although his legacy remains contested. The narrative of Jenner's groundbreaking work on smallpox prevention is far more nuanced than conventional historical accounts suggest.

In 1767, Dr. John Zephaniah Holwell presented his groundbreaking observations of Bengali smallpox inoculation practices to the Royal College of Physicians in London. His detailed account, "An Account of the Manner of Inoculating for the Smallpox in the East Indies," meticulously documented a sophisticated medical practice refined over centuries in India. Both the procedure and its efficacy was observed and tested by Holwell for nearly two decades prior to writing. The significance of his findings were so enormous that it earned him a Fellowship of the Royal Society. The ideas he presented were significant because they were not a part of the mainstream discussions and brought new information to the discourse.

First, he provided a comprehensive and precise illustration of the inoculation practice prevalent in India, offering valuable insights into a well-established method of developing immunity against smallpox. This documentation offered a profound look into the efficacy and long-term implementation of variolation techniques.

Second, his account served to legitimise and promote variolation within European medical communities. By highlighting its extensive use and effectiveness across non-European regions, Holwell bolstered confidence among European practitioners and paved the way for widespread acceptance of this preventive method.

Without Holwell's honesty in documenting at the time, it would have been unimaginable for us today to look at the scholarly discourse surrounding the origins of inoculation—a masterclass in academic obfuscation. One observes with remarkable fascination how researchers navigate the treacherous waters of medical historiography, carefully sidestepping the most obvious historical evidence with the precision of a diplomatic negotiator avoiding an uncomfortable truth.

Consider the intellectual ballet: distinguished academics document India's medical systems as the most ancient, explicitly acknowledging the antiquity of Ayurvedic practices. They also acknowledge India as a civilisation renowned for its sophisticated understanding of human physiology, surgical innovation, and holistic medical approaches. And yet, with a breathtaking display of cognitive gymnastics, they proceed to attribute the origins of inoculation to Turkey or China! The Indian antecedents of these practices are absent!

Where present, these foundational Indian practices—foundational even to the Turkish and Chinese—have been reduced to mere footnotes. Indian practices were often labeled as pagan or heathen rituals rather than recognized as legitimate scientific methods, obscuring a thorough and objective understanding of their genius and contributions.

The successive waves of invasions—particularly the Islamic invasions from the ninth century and later European colonisation—represented systematic intellectual decimation. Libraries in Nalanda, Taxila, and multiple scholarly centers were not merely destroyed but with it, thousands of manuscripts were burnt, scholars massacred, and entire knowledge transmission networks were brutally disrupted.

The medical knowledge around inoculation—a practice refined in India centuries before Western medicine—was transmitted through the Middle East, appropriated, and then reimagined as a European breakthrough. This wasn't just cultural theft; it was a sophisticated mechanism of intellectual colonisation where the colonised were simultaneously the original innovators and the most comprehensively silenced voices.

Despite the clear temporal sequence and the availability of multiple colonial accounts and works in medical circles, Jenner's contribution would be portrayed as a standalone European discovery. If anything, Jenner's development of vaccination was an innovation that built upon the existing practice of inoculation or variolation. The modern medical narrative is less a scientific chronicle and more a carefully constructed mythology of Western scientific supremacy.

This book seeks to rectify this historical injustice by highlighting the significant role Indian sciences played in the development of vaccination. It aims to reclaim the rightful place of these ancient Indian practices within the narrative of modern vaccine history, ensuring that their impacts are not just understood but fully appreciated.

The mission here transcends mere documentation. I hope it brings together medical researchers, Ayurvedic practitioners, and scholars to collaborate— challenge existing paradigms, petition peak bodies to update the literature, and ensure that future generations understand the depth and brilliance of Indian medical sciences— it is about reclaiming our intellectual sovereignty and inspiring a new generation to take pride in our scientific legacy.

Our knowledge is not a footnote. It is the cornerstone upon which modern medical understanding is built.

DIACRITICAL MARKS

When I began writing this book, Sanskrit diacritical marks were as foreign to me as they might be to many readers. My initial drafts used simplified spellings like 'Ayurveda' and 'Shitala.' However, as I delved deeper into my research, I discovered how these precise markings unlocked deeper meanings and connections within the texts I studied.

I came to appreciate that these diacritical marks are essential in academic contexts where precise pronunciation is necessary for understanding linguistic and textual nuances. For example, the distinction between śāstra (scripture/treatise) and shastra (weapon) carries significant semantic importance in Sanskrit texts.

For us as general readers, while exact pronunciation may not be crucial, understanding these marks helps appreciate the sophistication of Indic languages and their phonetic complexity. Common words like Āyurveda, Lakṣmī, or Śītalā carry these marks to preserve their authentic pronunciation.

Think of these marks as musical notations - they guide us to the true rhythm and melody of these ancient words. I've included a simple guide to help you navigate them. My hope is that as you journey through this book, these marked words will become familiar friends, just as they did for me, enriching your understanding of our Indian traditions.

Primary categories of diacritical marks used in this book are listed below:

Vowel Length Indicators

ā (as in āyurveda): indicates a prolonged 'a' sound, similar to the vowel in "father"

ī (as in Śrī): represents a prolonged 'ee' sound, as in "feet"

ū (as in mūla): denotes a prolonged 'oo' sound, as in "root"

Sub-script Notations

ṃ: represents the nasal sound (anusvāra)

ṇ: indicates the retroflex nasal consonant

ṣ: denotes the retroflex sibilant

ḍ: represents the retroflex 'd' sound

Special Consonant Markers

ś: represents the palatal sibilant (similar to 'sh')

ñ: indicates the palatal nasal sound

This standardized system of transliteration ensures consistency in academic writing and helps maintain the integrity of original Sanskrit and Indic pronunciations in Roman script.

CHAPTER 1

SUITCASES AND STILLNESS

Tārā's sobbing shattered the silence of the lockdown-laden household. "She's gone! Cremated in a black body bag like a nameless person! Is this what we've been reduced to?" Her voice, thick with sorrow, echoed through the rooms as she collapsed onto her bed, mourning her best friend's mother—another life claimed by the merciless coronavirus.

"Vaccine, vaccine, kuṭhe āhe te Vaccine?" she raged, her frustration palpable in every syllable. "When will this nightmare end?" The fire in her eyes matched the fury in her heart, directed at a healthcare system buckling under the weight of countless patients. Today, however, her anger gave way to a crushing sense of helplessness. Her best friend, forced to face her mother's illness and death in isolation—it was too much to bear.

Nana, engrossed in his book nearby, set it aside. He made his way to Tārā's bedside, his weathered hand coming to rest on her back in silent comfort.

It was the final blow that shattered her. After months of quiet endurance, Tārā's frustration erupted like a long-dormant volcano. Her dreams of studying in America—carefully nurtured over years, so tantalisingly close a few months ago—now seemed as distant as the stars.

Here she was, trapped in the very town she had been so eager to escape. Her packed bags—a mocking reminder of the derailed plans.

Of Nana's three grandchildren—Tārā, Bhuvaneśvarī, and Pārtha—she was undoubtedly the most spirited. Her fiery temperament had only intensified with age, and into her college years. Tārā had skilfully planted the seeds of wanderlust in her younger siblings as well. Their move to a nearby metropolis for college was part of her grand design.

As Nana comforted her, Tārā's ragged breathing gradually steadied. He silently rejoiced in having her home, even under these circumstances. *"Tārā Rānī,"* he said softly, "and even after we find one, it might be a while before the world is truly free of Corona's shadow."

"And just how long must we wait? Months? Years? Until all my plans turn to dust?" Tārā's voice cracked with frustration as she demanded an answer.

To Nana, Tārā was more than just a name hastily chosen from a family tree. In her, he saw the living spirit of Tārā rani, the formidable Maratha queen renowned for her strategic brilliance and military prowess. His granddaughter carried that same unshakeable fire—a flame that burned too bright sometimes, leading her to clash with anyone who stood in her path. Where the queen had commanded armies, young Tārā waged wars with sharp words and sharper principles, turning even minor disagreements into battles of honour. He watched her with pride tinged with concern, hoping life would teach her to wield her passion like a blade: knowing when to strike, and when to hold steady.

"I know this is not the answer you want to hear, but it could be decades, perhaps even centuries," Nana replied, drawing from his years of experience in the medical field. "It took us more than 180 years to eradicate smallpox, in 1980, since its first vaccine. Corona's reach is vast and this may be our new normal for a while."

He sat on the edge of her bed and patted her shoulder gently. "But do not lose heart, my dear. Science moves faster now. We may wake up any day to news of a breakthrough." His voice warmed with patriotic pride. "And who knows? Bhārat might even lead the charge in providing this vaccine to the world!"

Tārā scoffed, her disdain palpable. "Nana, what fantasy world are you living in? Aunty died because hospitals lack ventilators, doctors are without PPE, and both caregivers and patients are falling like flies in your beloved Bhārat! How can you expect this broken system to save us?" Her voice dripped with scepticism. "No thank you, we'll be waiting for Oxford or Harvard to ride to our rescue."

"Would it surprise you to learn that Bhārat has always possessed the knowledge to make this happen?" Nana countered. "In fact, our ancient wisdom laid the foundation for modern vaccination."

Tārā rolled her eyes. "Oh, please! You sound like that character from '*My Big Fat Greek Wedding*'—everything originated in Greece! Yes, India had a glorious past, but how does that help me now? I do not believe your 'Merā Bhārat Mahān' rhetoric when I see the reality around us."

"As well, you should not blindly believe!" Nana retorted. "*Satyam ca svādhyāya pravacane ca.* Bhārat can claim the foundations of vaccination before any other civilisation. But do not take my word for it."

As their conversation paused, both glanced at the clock. Nearly 7 PM—her cue to retreat. She dashed to her room, avoiding what was to come.

Nana smiled knowingly as he approached the *devghar*, lighting the *samaī*. Gone were the days when gathering the children for evening prayers was easy. Their affection remained, but their enthusiasm had waned. Soon, his resonant voice filled the house with the chants of the *Vishnu Sahasranama.*

Tārā shut her door, muffling Nana's voice. "First to find vaccination, my foot!" she muttered. "I'll show you the truth, just you wait."

CHAPTER 2

MORNING TEA STIRS A MEMORY

The sun's early rays filtered through the curtains, casting a neon glow across the room. Urmila stood by the window, basking in the warmth of a new day. Her lips moved in a quiet chant,

"oṃ bhāskarāya vidmahe
mahātejāya dhīmahi
tannaḥ sūryaḥ pracodayāt,"

the ancient *Surya Gayatri* rolling off her tongue with practised ease. It was a ritual as old as time, a connection to the cosmic dance that began each morning.

Urmila moved with practised efficiency, her hands working almost of their own accord as she prepared the first round of *chaha*. It was a morning ritual that usually enticed only the elders of the household. Her children typically surfaced hours later, just in time for breakfast and the second round of tea.

But today was different. As Urmila poured the steaming tea into delicate porcelain cups, a sleepy voice caught her off guard.

"*Āyī*, mine too."

Urmila turned to find Tārā, her eldest, standing in the doorway. Her eyes were still heavy with sleep, her hair a tangled mess atop her head. It was a rare sight to see her up this early.

"Are you feeling alright?" Urmila asked, concern colouring her voice as she reached for another cup.

Tārā nodded, stifling a yawn. "Hmm. I could not sleep. Thought I'd get an early start."

An hour later, when Urmila returned from her morning walk, she was surprised to find Tārā still at the table. Her daughter sat hunched over her laptop, completely engrossed in whatever had captured her attention.

"Put it away and come help me. *Khicaḍī taak...*," Urmila called out, gesturing towards the bowl of sābūdāṇā that had been soaking overnight. It was a favourite in their household, especially Tārā's. The prospect of her mother's *sābūdāṇā khicaḍī* usually had Tārā rushing to help, but today, she seemed distracted.

"Nah, you do the *khicaḍī*, I'll do the *khamaṅga kākaḍī*," Tārā replied, finally tearing her eyes away from the screen. She moved to the fridge, pulling out a handful of fresh cucumbers. As she began to peel them, a question seemed to weigh on her mind. "Āyī, do you know anything about smallpox?"

Urmila's hands stilled over the stove. "Why do you ask?"

"Nothing... just something Nana said," Tārā shrugged nonchalantly.

"Hmm..." Urmila sighed. "I know it all too well," she murmured. It made Tārā's skin prickle for she had rarely heard her Āyī speak with such... was it sorrow? Regret?

"Tell mummy, tell," Tārā insisted, unaware of the painful memories she was about to unearth.

Urmila was quiet for a long moment, gathering her thoughts. The sizzle of cumin seeds hitting hot oil filled the silence. When she finally spoke, her voice was soft, tinged with a sadness that made Tārā stop grating the cucumber and look up.

"You know how all of us sisters, brothers, and cousins grew up together in the big *wada*?" Urmila began, her eyes distant as she stirred the *khicaḍī*. "Well, one day, Chabu *ātyā* forbade us from entering her house. Her son, our youngest cousin, had been complaining of being tired. We thought he was just being naughty, trying to get out of his turn in the hide-n-seek game."

Urmila's voice faltered. "But he had a high fever. And then... the rash appeared. It spread everywhere - his face, arms, legs. In just a matter of days, it was... horrifying."

Tārā listened, transfixed, as her mother painted a vivid picture. She described how they would sneak to the window, peering in at their cousin sitting or lying on a mattress on the floor, covered only by a thin mul-mul cloth. His body was a battlefield, overrun by pustules that formed crusts, dried, and fell off.

"Chabu *ātyā* would shoo us away," Urmila continued, her voice barely above a whisper. "'If you do not want to end up like him, stay away,' she'd say. But we did not understand. We'd ask her, 'Then why are you near him?' And she'd yell back, 'I've already been through it; I have seen *Devī*.' It made no sense to us then."

Urmila explained how they did not understand about incubation periods, or that survivors gained lifelong immunity. They were just children, trying to make sense of a world suddenly turned upside down.

"We kept sneaking back to his window, trying to cheer him up," she said, her voice breaking. "Until one afternoon... he just was not there when we returned from school."

The kitchen fell silent. Tārā stood motionless, the half-grated cucumber forgotten in her hand. She watched as her mother wiped away a stray tear, the weight of the memory evident in the slump of her shoulders.

"Āyī," Tārā said softly, "the *khicaḍī* is done."

Urmila blinked, coming back to the present. She turned off the stove and faced her daughter. "So, what was it that Nana said?"

Tārā hesitated, "That India knew how to treat smallpox long before the West."

"And you do not believe him?" a knowing smile playing at her lips, Urmila asked.

Tārā shrugged. "I mean, if we did, would it not be common knowledge?"

Urmila smiled softly, some of the earlier heaviness lifting. "You know Nana... he rarely says things without reason. Taking him on means hard work. Are you game?"

Tārā grinned, her earlier skepticism morphing into curiosity. Urmila went on to remind her daughter of Nana's vast knowledge and interests, which had earned him the childhood nickname 'Nana' - meaning 'many' in Marathi. His real name, Dr Laxman Mavlankar, *Āyurveda Tīrtha*, was now limited to his letterhead.

As they finished cooking breakfast, Urmila shared how Nana had always treated her like the daughter he never had. From philosophical discussions to socio-political debates, nothing was off-limits in their conversations. It was Nana who had insisted she study law, often helping in the kitchen or taking the kids to the park so she could study or sit for exams.

"I'm a successful lawyer today because of his unconditional support," Urmila said, her voice warm with gratitude. "I know your Nana all too well, and the erudition you're challenging."

Tārā listened, a newfound respect for her grandfather blooming in her chest. As she topped the delicious hot *khicaḍī* with freshly grated coconut and coriander, she declared dramatically, "But with your *khicaḍī*, I can take on anybody!"

Chapter 3

NETOPEDIA TRIUMPHS

Tārā burst into Nana's room, her laptop clutched like a shield, eyes blazing with the fire of perceived victory. Little did she know, she would learn that history, like her grandfather, held more surprises than a Netopedia page could contain.

"You were wrong!" Tārā declared triumphantly, thrusting her laptop screen towards Nana. The Netopedia entry on Edward Jenner glowed on the screen, a digital testament to her hours of research.

Nana peered over his glasses, a bemused smile playing on his lips. "What about?" he asked, his voice calm in the face of his granddaughter's storm.

"India had ABSOLUTELY NOTHING to do with the smallpox vaccination!" Tārā emphasised, her voice ringing with the certainty of youth. "The first vaccine was developed by Edward Jenner. Look!"

As Nana settled in to listen, Tārā launched into a passionate recap of Jenner's life. Her words painted the picture of a curious orphan who, at just 13, apprenticed with a country surgeon near Bristol. She spoke of his varied interests — from geology to human blood, even his brief foray into ballooning.

"Did you know he was only 21 when he went to study under one of England's most famous surgeons?" Tārā's excitement was palpable. "He even assisted Captain Cook in classifying species from his first voyage!"

Nana listened intently as Tārā continued her tale, detailing Jenner's return to Berkeley to practice medicine. Her voice softened as she recounted the fateful words of a dairymaid: "I shall never have smallpox for I had cowpox."

"He found a young dairy maiden, Sarah Nelms, with fresh cowpox lesions," Tārā explained. "Using matter from her pustules, Jenner inoculated his gardener's son, 8-year-old James Phipps. James caught cowpox. Then for the next stage of the experiment, months later, he inoculated Phipps with smallpox. Guess what, no disease developed. Voila! Indeed if you have suffered cowpox, you do not suffer from smallpox. The dairy maiden was so right and the protection was complete."

As Tārā's narrative reached its peak, she noticed Nana's enigmatic smile. It was the same smile he wore when she was young and insisted the moon followed their car.

"Is it not strange," she mused, her certainty wavering, "that such noble efforts were met with resistance across Europe? The Royal Society even rejected his paper!"

Nana's eyes twinkled. "Indeed, Jenner's hard work paid off after a few decades of *tapasya*," he said, using the Sanskrit word deliberately.

Tārā pressed on, detailing how the vaccine spread to America, how Jenner received recognition and substantial grants from the British Parliament. "Did you know his work was considered of such extraordinary value that it was publicly acknowledged by the British Parliament in 1802? It awarded Edward Jenner £10,000 and additional £20,000 five years later!"

"I knew his work was significant," Nana said softly, "but I was not aware of the awards. I'm glad you found something to occupy your mind, Tārā Rānī. Stay a while and we'll talk more after *parvācā.*»

"Nah, you carry on. I just wanted to tell you...you got this one wrong. We'll talk later." She dashed off.

As the sound of *Vishnu sahasranama* filled the house, Tārā sat in her room, staring at her laptop. The Netopedia page still glowed on the screen. "Huh! This was easy — in fact, too easy. Nana did not even put up a fight," she thought.

Tārā's triumph curdled into doubt. Was this truly a victory, or had she stumbled into some elaborate trap of Nana's making? This was no quick win — it was the calm before a storm of revelations.

Chapter 4

Postcards from the Past

"*Chai, garam chai!*" Tārā's voice rang out as she entered Nana's room, carefully balancing his afternoon tea. Nana, roused from his *siesta*, gestured towards his study table. As Tārā set down the cup, her eyes caught a faded postcard with an unsettling image.

"What's this?" she asked, picking up the weathered card. The image depicted an Indian toddler covered with smallpox, identifying it as *'Devī'* and warning of its disfiguring, blinding, and often fatal effects.

"Ah, that Tārā Rānī, was the secret weapon in Bhārat's war against smallpox," Nana's eyes twinkled with pride. *'Bhārat Sarkār* offered a hundred rupees — a princely sum back then — to anyone who reported a fresh case. And as the disease began to retreat, the bounty grew. A marketing masterstroke, as you kids call it these days."

He chuckled, lost in memories. "You should have seen it. Loudspeakers in every *galli*, radio ads, TV spots, newspaper ads... Even the walls could not escape — plastered with posters promising riches for vigilant citizens. It was a fever pitch of awareness!"

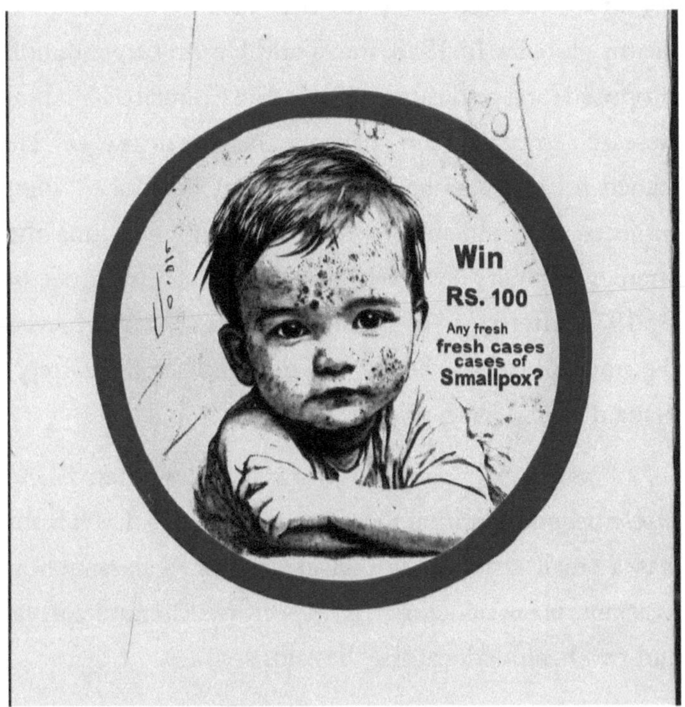

Nana's voice softened with a hint of nostalgia. "You see, Tārā, your old Nana was not just a bystander. I know a thing or two about that eradication effort. It was a time when every Indian became a foot soldier in the battle against smallpox. I was too."

Intrigued, Tārā settled beside Nana, her earlier skepticism forgotten. Nana's voice took on a reminiscent tone as he unveiled his personal connection to this historic effort.

"You see, back then, *Bhārat* was the world's epicenter for smallpox, accounting for over half of all cases and deaths globally. In 1958, the World Health Organisation proposed total eradication. The Indian Council of Medical Research embraced this challenge the very next year." He leaned forward, his hands animated as he spoke. "Pilot projects were initiated to determine and fine-tune the strategy, estimate costs, and determine manpower needs. By 1977, after years of relentless effort, *Bhārat* achieved the unthinkable — *Bhārat* was declared smallpox-free," Nana declared, with pride.

"I was just a young lad in my twenties when *Bhārat sarkar* began recruiting for vaccination teams. Each team was a small army: a supervising doctor, a paramedical assistant, 60 vaccinators, 12 inspectors, 12 enumerators, and two health educators," he said.

Nana's eyes twinkled mischievously. "You know, I impressed one of the supervising doctors with my enthusiasm and knowledge. I could explain the vaccination process better than seasoned professionals — using a rotary lancet, applying freeze-dried vaccine from 20-dose ampoules, with just one or two insertions per person. That's how I joined as a paramedical assistant," he continued. "For two years, I traversed every nook and cranny of the state, knocking on countless doors in our assigned areas. It was exhausting work, but every vaccinated person brought us closer to our goal."

As Nana immersed himself in the depths of his memories, a profound emotion welled up within him, causing his eyes to glisten with unshed tears. "What I saw on the ground, Tārā Rānī, is what made me study medicine," he said.

His mind drifted to the dilapidated shanty where a malnourished boy and his sister played hopscotch, their mother struggling to light a fire inside. The father, a daily wage earner, was away, leaving the family without supplies or money.

"I shared my meals with them that day," Nana said, his voice thick with emotion. He left out one tiny detail, that after returning to his dorm, he had sobbed with overwhelm. This was just one of many such families he had encountered. Born in colonial India, Nana too had great ideas of what a *swatantra Bhārat* would evolve into. The grim reality on the ground, two decades after independence had crushed his dreams like a wrecking ball.

Tārā sat in stunned silence as Nana reached for his now-lukewarm tea. She realised that sometimes, the most profound lessons come not from online searches, but from the stories buried in the hearts of those who lived them.

'How very Jenneresque, Nana!' Tārā thought out loud. Her eyes drifted to the glass showcase behind him, filled with awards and accolades, modestly tucked away from prying eyes. A wave of admiration washed over her.

Even though Nana had hung up his stethoscope over a decade ago, his reputation as a healer lived on. *Vaidyas*, doctors, medical students, and his former patients still sought his counsel. How many times had she witnessed the look of awe on a patient's face when Nana accurately described their symptoms just by checking their pulse? His gift for diagnosis was legendary. With every consultation, Nana dispensed not just treatment, but a potent blend of hope and wisdom. "Lead a simpler life," he'd say, "one that's in harmony with nature." Those words etched in her mind, his holistic approach to healing.

Some patients like Yashoda would walk for miles, from beyond the villages and remote tribal areas, to get to him. He had a soft corner for such patients. He welcomed them, gave them water and *gul*, and asked them to rest a while under the mango tree. Tārā recalled running into the kitchen to announce, "*Āyī*, Yashoda is here." The women of the house knew to prepare additional meals that Urmila dutifully served to Yashoda. Only after a hearty meal would Nana examine them, give them not only medicines but also money to take a bus back home. To him, the fees he received as the basketful of *jāmbūla* or a jackfruit that Yashoda had carried on her head all the way into town, was more valuable than money.

A realisation struck her like a thunderbolt. Here she'd been, mooning over Jenner, blind to the giant before her. Nana's whole life had been in service to the neediest, bridging ancient and modern healing arts. How had she missed it?

"Nana, your tea has gone cold. Let me reheat it for you," abruptly she left the room, mind reeling. She needed time to comprehend the uneasiness that invaded her.

CHAPTER 5

THE DIVINE DELIVERANCE

. . . .

The fragrance of *agarbatti* swirled in the air, carrying with it Nana's reverence.

kāyena vācā manasendriyairvā

buddhyātmanā vā prakṛtisvabhāvāt

karomi yadyat sakalam parasmai

nārāyaṇāyeti samarpayāmi

His voice, weathered by time yet strong with devotion, filled the small room. As the final words of his prayer faded, Nana's eyes opened to find Tārā sitting quietly beside him, her presence as unexpected as it was welcome.

"How long have you been here? I did not hear you come in!" Nana exclaimed, his surprise evident.

Tārā's lips curved into a gentle smile. "You were too engrossed," she said, her gaze drawn to the serene *devghar*.

Pulling up a chair beside him in front of the *devghar*, her muscle memory kicked in as she bowed and offered *namaskar*. "I have a question about this," she said waving the postcard with the smallpox ad. "So why was this disease called *Devī* in the first place?" Tārā's fingers traced its worn edges.

"Hmm...Do you remember the stories I told you when you were little?" Nana asked.

Tārā's blank expression spoke volumes.

"Well, think about it. In our stories, whenever we faced insurmountable obstacles or when demons wreaked havoc on this planet, a powerful goddess – a Devī – would appear. Devī Vishnumaya slew demons Madhu and Kaidabha. As Durga, she killed Mahishasura. And as Chandika, she decapitated Shumbha and Nishumbha."

Tārā leaned forward, her curiosity piqued. "But what does that have to do with smallpox?"

"Smallpox, my dear Tārā Rānī, was a demon in its own right, an insurmountable demon," Nana explained, his voice taking on a somber tone. "A disease potent enough to wipe out entire civilisations across the globe. Its origins are lost in the mists of time, but some believe it appeared in the first agricultural settlements more than 10,000 years ago."

As Nana spoke, Tārā's mind raced, connecting dots. "I've briefly read about how many populations around the world went extinct due to this disease," she interjected.

"Extinct or exterminated?" he asked sharply. Nana let his words hang in the air for a second before moving on.

"Anyway, so yes the impact of smallpox on history is far greater than most realise. It holds some dark chapters now carefully buried in the sands of time, Tārā Rānī. But that is a story for another time."

A chill ran down Tārā's spine as she thought to herself, "I am not sure if I want to find out more."

"In Europe, well into the 18th century about 4 lakh people were dying of smallpox each year, and nearly one-third of that number also went blind. But you see, Tārā, that's where our *Bhārat's* wisdom comes in."

Tārā's brow furrowed. "You mean... India had a solution?"

"Not just a solution. We had an entire system of knowledge, personified in a goddess herself," Nana said with a hint of pride. "Śītalā.»

Tārā quickly pulled out her phone, her fingers flying over the screen. "I found her! She looks... different from our usual *Devīs*. No jewelry, just some very simple red or light blue saree. She's holding some kind of pointy broom in one hand and a small pot in the other. And... is that a *soupli* in her hair? And she's riding a donkey? How peculiar!" she exclaimed, showing Nana the image.

Nana chuckled with amusement. "Excellent, Sherlock! Now remember, with our *Devīs* and *Devatās*, you need to look beyond the literal. Think of it as a concept. Tell me, what comes to mind when I ask you to visualise an *ākāśakandīl*?"

"Why, of course Diwali! Our whole house lit up, early morning firecrackers, *pharāl*, shopping, celebrating with friends." A broad smile flashed across her face as she described her favourite time of the year.

"You see how that one image of *ākāśakandīl* represents so many other associations? Same is the case with images of *Devīs* and *Devatās* with one additional complexity — they are multi-dimensional and open to more than one interpretation."

As Nana explained the symbolism behind Śītalā's iconography, Tārā's eyes opened to a new dimension. The patient burning with fever, managing it with cold water bath, the winnowing fan and broom – all representations of ancient medical knowledge and practices.

"I see. And why in the world does she ride a donkey? The most disliked and spurned of all animals?" Tārā asked, as she gathered all the information.

"There is deep meaning there as well, Tārā rani. We call a donkey 'gadha'. It comes from the Sanskrit word 'gardabha.' But here's what's significant - the word 'gardabhaka' has a dual meaning. It also describes a specific skin condition - one that manifests as round, red, painful spots."

Tārā leaned in, listening intently.

"They're like sarcoids - tumors commonly found on donkeys and horses. These sarcoids are dry, scaly masses that ulcerate and bleed, appearing very similar to smallpox pustules. They typically show up on a donkey's head, chest, and shoulders during spring and early summer - the same seasons when smallpox would traditionally strike our villages."

"So by depicting Śītalā riding a donkey..." Tārā started piecing together the puzzle.

"The iconography shows Śītalā devi's mastery over the disease. It represents her control over the affliction itself. This is how our ancestors preserved crucial medical knowledge within our sacred imagery."Nana concluded.

"So the Western interpretation..."

"Missed this nuance entirely. But for us, she's more of a..." Nana paused, searching for the right words, "...a healing presence or mechanism."

Nana reached into the drawer beneath the *devghar* and pulled out an old Sanskrit book. Its rough red hardcover and tattered pages spoke of many readings over the years. Carefully flipping through the fragile pages, he handed her a chapter.

"*Śītalāshtakam?*"

Nana nodded encouragingly. "Look at the 5th *shloka.*»

Tārā's eyes scanned the Sanskrit verse:

"शीतलेज्वरदग्धस्यपूतिगन्धयुतस्यच।

प्रणष्टचक्षुषःपुंसस्त्वामाहुर्जीवनौषधम्॥५॥"

"*śītale jvaradagdhasya pūtigandha yutasya ca*

praṇaṣṭa cakṣuṣa puṃsastvamahurjīvanauṣadham" Nana recited, his voice resonating with the *shloka.* "It means: Oh Goddess, who is cool, it is told that you are the only living medicine for the one who is affected by high fever, and to the one who has bad smelling wounds, and also to the one who has lost his eyes."

"This is... incredible," Tārā sat back, overwhelmed by the depth of knowledge hidden beneath the simple facade.

"Then why does no one else know about this?" Her confusion turned to frustration.

"For centuries our rich and complex history has been written by those who came to destroy it. It is bound to be overshadowed by narratives that do not tell the full story," Nana replied.

As the evening deepened, Nana shared more about Śītalā Devī – how she was accompanied by Jvarasura, Oladevi, Ghentu-debata, and Raktabati, each representing different diseases and healing. He spoke of Śītalā Ashtami being celebrated on the eighth day after Holi, a festival that aligned with the seasonal patterns of smallpox occurrence.

"Even the timing of her worship was based on a deep understanding of the seasonal patterns," Nana explained. "Practitioners knew that mortality rates were high during the hot and dry months from February through May, declining with the onset of monsoon in June. That's why smallpox was colloquially known as *Basantaroga* – the spring disease."

Tārā absorbed this wealth of information, knowing she had opened Pandora's box.

Chapter 6

Conquest Through Contagion

Tārā's fingers trembled as she read the final words on her screen: 'I hope it will have the desired effect.'

She scrolled back up, refusing to believe what she'd just read. But there it was, documented in stark black and white: William Trent, a militia commander, had deliberately handed over two blankets and a handkerchief from a smallpox hospital to visiting Native American chiefs.

Her stomach churned as she discovered an entire correspondence between General Jeffery Amherst and Colonel Bouquet, its casual cruelty preserved in perfect cursive: "Could it not be contrived to send the Smallpox among those disaffected tribes of Indians? We must on this occasion use every stratagem in our power to reduce them."

Reduce them. As if they were numbers in an equation, not human beings.

Her cursor hovered over the date - June 22, 1763. Fort Pitt stood at the meeting point of three rivers, where Pittsburgh now sprawled. She could picture it: 330 British soldiers and civilians, barricaded inside while Delaware warriors surrounded them.

In Colonel Bouquet's own words, "every Tree is become an Indian" – a line that made Tārā pause. It revealed sophisticated tactics of the Native American warriors. The Delaware and other tribes melted into forests only to emerge again in surprise attacks.

Their strategic brilliance had the British on the verge of defeat, their traditional military logic useless against indigenous warfare. But instead of fighting with muskets and cannons, the British commanders - Colonel Henry Bouquet and Captain Simeon Ecuyer - turned a disease into a weapon.

The screen's glow illuminated her face as she fell deeper into the rabbit hole of research. The numbers struck her like physical blows: 30% to 90% of Native populations, wiped out across various regions in the Americas. Not by swords, not by guns, but by invisible enemies they had no immunity for, no defense against.

She found accounts from Delaware elders, passed down through generations, speaking of the "great dying." Their stories told of medicine men and healers watching helplessly as the mysterious illness ravaged their people, their traditional remedies powerless against this new enemy. The devastating loss was not just of lives, but of knowledge - each elder who died took with them centuries of oral history, cultural practices, and traditional medicine.

Her fingers flew across the keyboard, and each new search revealed a prior horror. The Spanish in Mexico, watching as smallpox devastated Tenochtitlan in the 1520s, killing the Aztec emperor Cuitláhuac and leaving the mighty city a necropolis. Forty percent of the population, gone in a single year. Aztec codices spoke of bodies piling in streets once filled with market vendors and children's laughter, of temples falling silent, of a civilization brought to its knees not by conquistadors' steel, but by invisible spores on traded blankets and shared breath.

"Oh god," she whispered, her hand covering her mouth as she reached the Australian chapter. 1789, just one year after the First Fleet dropped anchor in Port Jackson. The Eora people - the Cadigal, Bidjigal, and Cammeraygal clans - had fished and hunted in Sydney's waters for millennia. Within months of the British arrival, smallpox tore through their communities. Fifty to seventy percent of them vanished.

A marine officer named Watkin Tench had recorded the apocalyptic scene in 1791. His words burned themselves into Tārā's mind: "The poor wretches were everywhere lying dead or dying along the shore, on the points of the rocks, in caverns of the stone, and deserted houses, and the natives were crawling like animals out of the woods to find water and food."

She found oral histories from Eora descendants, speaking of their ancestors' memories of that time. They told of finding entire family groups in their bark shelters, silent and still. Of children orphaned, of sacred sites abandoned, of songlines broken as those who carried the ancient stories succumbed one by one. The survivors spoke of watching their loved ones' bodies change, of the helplessness of not understanding why their traditional healing practices could not save them.

The British settlers had recorded it all with clinical detachment, protected by their immunity while they watched entire Indigenous villages empty of life. Some even saw it as divine providence, clearing the land for their use. Their letters home spoke of newly vacant territories, ripe for settlement, as if the land had simply emptied itself for their convenience.

The systematic use of disease as a weapon, the calculated genocide masked as 'providence', the clinical documentation of entire peoples being erased. This was not just a weapon, but a tool for colonisation. What better way to claim a land than to first empty it of its people? And then to write the history books claiming these deaths were inevitable, natural, divine providence?

Tārā slammed her laptop shut, her hands shaking. Suddenly the room felt too small, too stuffy. She needed air. Rising abruptly from her desk, she walked to the window and pushed it open, letting the cool evening breeze wash over her face.

CHAPTER 7

HOLWELL'S EASTERN ACCOUNT

. . . .

"Inoculation was practised in India from the remotest antiquity. It is in the hands of a particular tribe of Bramins;" Wait what...Tārā could not believe what she had stumbled upon.

"*Āyī*, look! Brindavan, Banaras, and Allahabad had colleges where Brahmins knew how to treat people against smallpox before Jenner!!" She felt electricity coursing through her veins, the kind of thrill that only came with discovering something that upended everything you knew.

Urmila looked up from arranging papers in her court briefcase. "An Account of the Manner of Inoculating for the Small Pox in the East Indies," Tārā read aloud, her voice carrying a sense of reverence "By J.Z. Holwell."

"Aga, but did you not want to prove Nana wrong? Is this not proving him right instead?" Urmila was amused.

"Tchh... You're missing the point! *Jāū de*," Tārā waved her hand dismissively, diving back into her research.

The story unfolded before her eyes. John Zephaniah Holwell, a Dublin-born surgeon who'd arrived in Bengal with the British East India Company in the mid-18th century. She pictured him, fresh off the boat, probably expecting to find medical practices primitive compared to Europe's. Instead, he'd witnessed something extraordinary.

Holwell's _An Account of the Manner of Inoculating for the Small Pox in the East Indies_ (1767) was one of the earliest accounts and the most detailed account to describe the Indian practice of variolation also called inoculation.

He spent several decades in Bengal, working in various capacities, including as a governor of Fort William in Calcutta. His most notorious experience was during the Siege of Calcutta when he was imprisoned by Nawab Siraj-ud-Daulah in what became known as the "Black Hole of Calcutta." But this did not deter his interest in India, and he continued to explore the medical practices.

He witnessed four major smallpox epidemics during his time in Bengal. This is where he observed the practice of inoculation by the Brahmins. Initially skeptical of this practice of inoculation, he eventually became convinced of its efficacy after observing its consistent success.

"Listen to this, they had it down to a science! And even had a whole system of preparation and aftercare!" Tārā spoke with excitement without even realising Urmila had left the room.

She scrolled further, reading about how Holwell's medical training and practice had enabled him to critique existing European medical practices in relation to smallpox treatment and advocates for the adoption of the cool regimen and open-air approach as practised in Bengal.

"Imagine being so convinced by something that you'd write a whole treatise about it, knowing your colleagues back home might ridicule you," Tārā mused, thinking about Holwell writing his account in 1767, decades before Jenner would even begin his research.

Though his account received mixed reviews in Europe, it remains significant for its role in the global history of smallpox inoculation, providing earliest and most detailed documentation of a practice that predated Edward Jenner's vaccine.

She opened a new document and began taking notes as it was getting too much to keep track of. This was not just about proving Nana wrong anymore. This was about understanding how knowledge flowed across centuries and continents, how modern discoveries often build on long forgotten ancient sciences.

Urmila, dressed in her crisp white saree with a black coat folded over her arm, reappeared at the doorway. "You're in charge of everyone's lunch. It's your favourite *masūrchi oosal*. Do not forget to get the *dahī* and *tāk* out of the fridge and clean up after. And tell me all about your discovery after I'm back."

"Ahhaha... *dhābbā* style *akkhā masūr with garam garam bhākrī!* I love you, Āyī!» Tārā's mouth watered at the thought of her favorite lentil dish. "Yes, boss!" She gave Urmila a seated salute and dug back into the reading.

The same year that he wrote this account, Holwell was elected as a Fellow of the Royal Society. Tārā read that this was the oldest known scientific academy in continuous existence. The Fellowship was a significant honour reserved for the very best in the field of science, medicine, engineering and technology. Legends like Ramanujan, Bose and Newton were some of the famous fellows.

This prestigious fellowship was awarded for Holwell's significant contributions to medical science and his pioneering study of Indian culture - most notable scientific achievement was his detailed description of smallpox variolation practices in 18th century Bengal!

"Wow! So his observations and written account was considered a groundbreaking, medical, and scientific contribution!"

Holwell conducted a 20-years long cohort study on smallpox inoculation in India, comparing outcomes between inoculated and uninoculated populations. This work, presented in his lecture to the Royal College of Physicians of London in 1767, demonstrated the efficacy of the Indian method of inoculation, showing that 90% of those inoculated survived subsequent epidemics, while 90% of the uninoculated perished. His research contributed to the understanding of early inoculation techniques.

Tārā's jaw dropped to the floor as she realised how important this contribution was to Europe's understanding and to further the development of vaccine technology back then. Here she was, frustrated about delayed dreams of studying abroad, while discovering that some of the most significant knowledge had flowed in the opposite direction. The Europeans, for all their colonial superiority, had found themselves learning from the very people they sought to subjugate!

The silence in the room was filled with unspoken questions. If a written account can be considered worthy of such prestige, what bevy of awards must be conferred on the knowledge system that created such a system? Or on the practitioners who kept this science alive against centuries of invasions? Why do I know so much about Holwell, Jenner, and all of the colonial exploits, yet nothing about the genius of my people who created it? How many other sophisticated Indian practices are out there? What other scientific achievements lay buried under centuries of colonial narrative?

Tārā was vexed with the idea that Bhārat's contributions have been erased from sight.

CHAPTER 8

BRINDAVAN-BENARAS BRAHMINS

Urmila was in high-spirits. A legal battle that had dragged on for eight long years was adjudicated in her clients favour. She returned with a box of *pedha* and offered them to everyone in the house along with the victory update.

The aroma of fresh tea mingled with the sweet scent of *pedhas* as Urmila set down a celebratory box of sweets.

"Now, what got you so animated earlier on?" Urmila asked, settling into her chair while Nana joined them, accepting a *pedha* with a warm smile.

"Oh I do not even know where to start!" Tārā replied.

"Best to start at the beginning then..."Urmila prodded.

"Well, I've been reading Dr. Holwell's account of smallpox inoculation. I never thought I'd say this about some medical research, but it's absolutely fascinating. This account was presented at a college of Physicians three decades before Jenner's vaccination, and the Indian treatment was being delivered centuries before!"

She described how Holwell had documented the cyclical nature of smallpox in Bengal - five to six years of mild occurrences followed by a devastating seventh-year epidemic that spared neither Indian nor European lives.

"But here's the incredible part," Tārā leaned forward, her voice dropping conspiratorially. "The Brahmin inoculators would actually ask parents, 'How many pocks would you like your child to have?' And they could control it! Unbelievable! And…get this, they used previous years pus material to generate the pocks! "Her hands moved animatedly as she spoke, a trait she'd inherited from her mother.

"Oh! So precision in medicine is not a western invention then?" Urmila said rhetorically, stirring her tea and Tārā.

Tārā glossed over her remark and continued describing the meticulous preparation - the month-long dietary restrictions, the careful skin preparation, the mixing of year-old smallpox matter with *Gaṅgājala*. Her voice grew more animated as she added the details.

They had this incredibly precise method - boys were inoculated between wrist and elbow, girls near the shoulder. Before the actual inoculation, they'd rub the skin with a cloth for about ten minutes, just to get the blood flowing. Then, with a small tool, they'd make tiny scratches and put a cotton swab with smallpox matter on it, mixed with *Gaṅgājala*.. They'd cover it with a bandage, and that was that—the inoculation was done!

They gave the families strict aftercare instructions. Every morning, they had to pour cold water over the child from head to toe, continuing until a fever appeared, which usually happened around the sixth day. Once the fever showed up, they stopped the cold baths for a while and then restarted them when the rash appeared. The cold water helped push the sickness out of the body and into the skin.

"Hence, *Śītalā*, literally meaning the one who cools," Nana interjected using air quotes for "cool", doing an impression of Tārā.

"Bingo!" she squealed. "I mean, I got it...I get it now," Tārā's voice dropped for a moment. But she did not linger there for long and continued adding details to the emerging picture.

Nana listened with a knowing smile. Urmila admiringly watched this exchange. She knew Tārā would find it hard to accept defeat and this was her way of saying so without the formality of it.

"An important part of the after care protocol was that as soon as the poxes started to change colour, they'd open them with a thorn—yes, a prickly thorn! The Bramins would also tell families to give the child cooling foods like bananas, sugarcane, and light drinks like rice water.

And...and get this-The inoculator recited *shlokas* the whole time, making it a sacred act. I'm starting to see how turning Śītalā into a *Devi* and ritualising the treatment became a way of ensuring that people strictly followed the inoculator's instructions." Tārā concluded her monologue.

"You have not said anything Nana," Urmila nudged Nana.

"Tārā Rānī has said it all today!" Nana affectionately gave her a pat on the back and smiled.

"I am glad that she has found the *Banaras brahmins*. The open secret no one wants to talk about! Their approach to inoculation was extremely efficient yet so strikingly different from European methods, which is why it was important enough for Holwell to write in such detail.

While European doctors were still struggling with fresh smallpox matter, causing severe reactions and sometimes death. *Bhārat's* method was refined over centuries with understanding of some key concepts, thanks to *Āyurveda*. This was not just tradition; it was science. " Nana reflected as he spoke.

All the names swirled around in Tārā's head... Holwell, Jenner, Phipps, Nelms anyone who was even slightly connected to this story had a name and place in the annals of history - Yet we know not a single name of the Brindavan, Banaras, and Allahabad Brahmins who went from morning until night, from door to door, performing such great service for a paltry fee of "a pund of *cowries*.»

CHAPTER 9

FROM INOCULATION TO VACCINATION

The warm glow of the laptop screen illuminated Tārā's face, her eyes wide with a mixture of disbelief and excitement. Her fingers trembled slightly as she scrolled through the letter, written centuries ago, that was about to shatter her preconceptions.

Tārā's fingers traced across the words of Reverend Charles Chais, a Protestant French church pastor, whose 1754 tract _Essai Apologetique held unexpected treasures. The document, predating Holwell's address, was more than just another European account – it was an inadvertent attestation to India's medical mastery.

"The variolous matter was preserved in a twisted thread," she read aloud, absorbing the account from Mr. D, the Reverend's Amsterdam correspondent. The description of an English widow's children receiving treatment at Fort William, Calcutta was meticulous. The Bengali inoculator passess a needle between flesh and skin to inoculate. Most remarkably, the inoculator informs us that he possessed material preserved from his grandfather's time, suggesting a sophisticated preservation system spanning generations.

An additional revelation came through yellowed pages of the online archives.

"The operation of inoculation called by the natives *tikah* has been known in the Kingdom of Bengal as nearly as I can learn for about 150 years..." Tārā's voice barely above a whisper like she had stumbled upon a secret.

The words of Robert Coult, penned on February 10, 1731, from Bengal to Dr. Oliver Coult in Britain, danced before her eyes. "...and according to the Bhaminian records, was first performed by one Dunuantary, a physician of Champanager, a small town by the side of Ganges about halfway to Cossimbazar, whose memory is now holden in great esteem as being thought the author of this operation, which secret, say they, he had immediately of a God in the dream."

150 years before 1731! So this is going all the way back to 1581!

"Dunuantary from Champanager!" Tārā chuckled at the British writer's misunderstanding. Even a lay person like her caught the discrepancy. Her mind drifted to the striking *murti* in Nana's dispensary she'd passed countless times without truly seeing. *Bhagavān Dhanvantari*, the physician of the Gods, stood serene, his divine form holding the precious *amṛta kalaśa*. His sage-like appearance embodied both eternal wisdom and compassion – the very essence of healing. The *janwa (janeu)* across his chest, the flowing locks of hair, and those knowing eyes seemed to hold secrets of the universe's medicine within them.

Where Coult had documented a single physician named "Dunuantary" receiving divine knowledge in a dream, he had actually stumbled upon something far more profound. Generation after generation of healers were known as *Dhanvantari* in reverence to this very deity, much like modern doctors took the Hippocratic oath.

Her amusement gave way to astonishment. Right before her was irrefutable evidence documented by Europeans themselves. Indians had been treating smallpox since the 15th century, with a well-developed understanding of the disease's patterns, multiple accurate treatment methods, and a system to preserve the highly infectious treatment material for generations.

She could not delay the inevitable any longer. With feigned casualness, Tārā strolled into Nana's room, her laptop clutched to her chest like a shield.

"You were right, you know," she murmured, her voice barely audible.

"What was that, Tārā Rānī?" Nana's eyes twinkled with mischief, betraying that he had heard her perfectly but was pretending otherwise.

Tārā sighed dramatically. "You were kinda right, but how is it my fault that this information is not on any of the main websites? I mean, who is going to do all this digging, as I did?" She looked at Nana expectantly, but he merely waited, patient as ever. He had played this cat-and-mouse game with Tārā for years and knew it well.

"Alright, alright," Tārā finally conceded, her words tumbling out in a rush. "You were right all along, and Bhārat was successfully treating smallpox, three centuries before Jenner's vaccine. There, I've said it. Happy now?"

With the hardest part out of the way, Tārā's enthusiasm took over. She regaled Nana with her findings from the past couple of days, her hands gesticulating wildly as she spoke.

"But Nana," she said, her brow furrowing, "I'm totally confused now. The internet tells me that inoculation was a high-risk procedure and Jenner made it safe with vaccination. What am I missing?"

"Yes it was high risk, within the European context. Here in Bhārat, *tikah* was being safely administered and smallpox material stored for centuries. Consider this," Nana settled into his teaching mode. "Europe had observed the dairy maidens' immunity, yes. But observation is not understanding. They saw the what but did not grasp the how or why. The concept of deliberately introducing a weaker infection to prevent a stronger one – that was not part of European medical thinking."

"But that's exactly what our inoculators were doing!" Tārā exclaimed.

"Precisely," Nana nodded. "The Indian method demonstrated something revolutionary to European medicine – that immunity could be induced artificially. This was not just about technique; it was also about understanding the body's ability to learn from controlled exposure."

"So when Jenner finally began his work..."

"He had few crucial but missing pieces of knowledge - the Indian principles of induced immunity as well as attenuated infections. Without understanding that controlled infection could create protection, the cowpox observation might have remained just that – an observation.»

Tārā sat up straighter, pieces clicking into place. "Aah...so by 1796, reports of Indian inoculation had been circulating in Europe for decades. Physicians like Holwell had documented everything from the preparation methods to the timing of procedures. This knowledge had time to percolate through medical circles."

"And influence thinking," Nana added. "Today you can print anything – t-shirts, mugs, even 3D heart valves and entire houses. But would any of that be possible without understanding the fundamental principles of printing? Similarly, vaccination needed the conceptual groundwork that Indian inoculation provided."

"We had the original knowledge that Jenner modified for his time and place!" Tārā exclaimed, remembering all the educational videos crediting Sarah Nelms and John Phipps, while the centuries of work by *Brindaban* and *Banaras brahmins* remained unmentioned. "The Bengal inoculators had already solved the primary puzzle – so Jenner's genius was not in discovering the principle..."

"But in finding a method to apply it," Nana completed her thought. "Using cowpox instead of smallpox was innovative, but it built upon centuries of Indian understanding of treating and managing smallpox with great success."

All the educational videos she had researched flashed before her eyes. They reminded viewers that not just Jenner but the dairy maiden Sarah Nelms' and the young boy John Phipps' contributions to the great cause should not be forgotten. Yet, no education video or website had even in passing mentioned the *Brindaban* and *Banaras brahmins* who had successfully treated the disease for centuries prior.

Tārā sank into her chair, the weight of this realisation settling heavily on her shoulders. Nana's words echoed in the background, "The British wrote what they saw through their colonial spectacles. As they say, history is written by the victors. Bear in mind, that does not make it the truth. It is just their version of the story. The truth is eternal, waiting for you to realise it."

CHAPTER 10

DIGESTED DISCOVERIES

The evening light cast long shadows as Nana entered his room for *parvācā*, finding Tārā by the window. Her laptop screen glowed dimly, illuminating her troubled expression. The familiar fragrance of *agarbattī* soon filled the air, his deep chanting creating a sacred cocoon around them both.

Drawn by the rhythm of the *Vishnu sahasranama*, Tārā quietly settled beside him, her troubled eyes finding peace in the steady flame of the *samaī*. As the chanting progressed, her breathing steadied, though the storm within had not fully subsided.

"What troubles my *shur-veer* Tārā Rānī?" Nana's gentle question came after the prayers, his hand resting affectionately on her shoulder. The patience in his silence invited her turmoil to surface.

"Erasure!, Nana," Tārā replied, despondently gesturing at her laptop screen where multiple browser tabs displayed historical documents. "It's the deliberate diminishing of the very knowledge they benefited from! And I think I understand why now – acknowledging India's contribution would have undermined their entire colonial narrative of civilising the 'primitive' East."

She clicked through to Dr. James Kirkpatrick's 1761 book "An Analysis of Inoculation," her voice tight with controlled anger. "Look at this pattern. They could not deny the effectiveness of our methods – there were too many witnesses, too much documentation. So instead, they did something more insidious. They separated the knowledge from its source."

Her fingers flew across the keyboard, pulling up more evidence. "They treated our medical advancement like a lucky accident – as if centuries of systematic observation and documentation meant nothing. According to these writers, it was the European 'scientific mind' that supposedly recognised the value in our 'primitive practices.'"

Nana's silence acknowledged her pain, a shared pain, and a deep ache in his heart.

"Listen to this – he reduced Bengal's sophisticated thread technique to a footnote! And then had the audacity to write, 'tho we give entire credit to the English lady, and equal credit to her Indian Dr is not a necessary consequence.'" Her voice quivered with indignation. "The English lady getting her children inoculated somehow outweighed centuries of indigenous medical expertise that kept the English children alive, when their peers were dying back home!"

"Elsewhere they wrote that 'this wonderful invention was found out not by the learned sons of erudition, but by mean, course, rude sort of people.'" She practically spat out the words. "Then, in 1758, a British columnist had the sheer audacity to declare 'England may be termed the native country of inoculation.' How? How could they claim this when their own documents prove it came from Bhārat?"

Her hands shook as she read from another document: "An encyclopedist in 1810 claimed inoculation was 'originally received from the hands of ignorance and barbarism.' He actually praised their 'learned countrymen' for not measuring 'the value of the practice by the meanness of its origins.'"

Tārā's voice rose with each revelation. "Ignorance and barbarism? These same people experimented on six Newgate prisoners and five Westminster orphans before treating their royalty! While they took four decades to extend treatment beyond their elite, our barbers, garland makers, astrologers, and vaidyas were treating everyone!"

She pulled out more documentation, her voice steadying as she cited the evidence: "Dr. Edward Ives's observations in Bengal in 1755, Dr. Francis Buchanan's witness accounts from Dinajpur in 1808 – both Hindu and Muslim cultivators serving as inoculators. Reverend Ward noted Daivajnas performing inoculations in 1822. In Dacca, 1840, garland makers and barbers were the practitioners. Risley even documented in 1891 that barbers possessed a textbook called 'Vasant-tika'!"

Nana watched thoughtfully, but his immediate concern was Tārā's growing distress. Her awakening to colonial historical manipulation needed guidance toward constructive understanding rather than consuming bitterness.

Quietly, he rose to switch on the ceiling fan, letting the cool breeze help temper her heated emotions. She would process this better once the initial shock subsided. His presence offered silent support – not dismissing her justified anger but providing an anchor of stability.

Tārā felt the subtle shift in atmosphere. Through her turmoil, she recognized Nana's careful handling of her emotional state. "What would I do without him?" she thought, a fresh wave of anxiety washing over her about eventually leaving for her studies.

As the breeze cooled her flushed cheeks, Tārā's righteous anger began transforming into something more purposeful. These digital archives were not just evidence of historical injustice – they revealed a deliberate pattern of intellectual colonisation.

Every dismissive footnote, every patronising acknowledgment was part of a larger narrative that justified colonial rule by denying indigenous achievement.

CHAPTER 11

FROM INDIA TO ITALY VIA ISTANBUL

"This can not be right," she muttered, scrolling through yet another article dismissing India's contribution to smallpox treatment. According to these sources, the earliest documentation, the inoculation practices came from China and Turkey.

The Ottoman practice of inoculation – where elderly women would collect year-old scabs from smallpox victims and insert them into small cuts on healthy people's arms. Another account spoke of Chinese physicians grinding smallpox scabs into powder and blowing them into patients' nostrils, a practice dated to the 1600s. Both sources definitively claimed these as the earliest documented forms of inoculation.

According to these papers, the scientific foundations of vaccination began with Turkish inoculation reaching Europe through Lady Mary Montagu's letters. "How is this possible? No mention of India anywhere?" Everything she was learning from her own deep dive – its sophisticated methodology, its widespread practice, multiple accounts, transmission of these accounts to Europe and its venture contributions to vaccination – none of this appeared in any of the mainstream articles. In the instances that it did, it was a passing mention.

"Tārā, take this to Nana" Urmila's voice broke through her concentration as she instructed Tārā to deliver Nana's breakfast to his room. It was the one day of the week that he did not come to the dining table.

Tārā welcomed the interruption. Sunday mornings were sacred – Nana's private time, a ritual that had started years ago when *Ājī* would watch *Ramayana* and *Mahabharata* with him. Though Ājī was gone now, the sanctity of Sunday mornings remained.

"Not watching *Mahabharata* rerun for the 100th time Nana?" Tārā teased him.

"No. Because I am looking for something I want to show you." She found Nana buried in books instead of watching his usual *Mahabharata* rerun. "Looking for something specific?" she asked, setting down his breakfast tray.

"Actually, yes." He gestured to the pile of books on his desk. "Open the top one."

"Let me grab my breakfast first!" She returned moments later with her iḍlī-sāmbhār, picking up the indicated book. "*Madhavanidana* by *Madhavakara*," she read aloud.

"You see, our ancestors had a brilliantly simple way of naming things," Nana began. "They called smallpox *'Masūrikā.'* Can you guess why?"

"Because it looked like *masūr daal*?" Tārā ventured, immediately regretting the comparison.

"Exactly! The eruptions resembled *masūr*, a lentil that was a staple across the subcontinent." Nana's eyes twinkled as Tārā pushed away her breakfast, suddenly losing her appetite.

"But that's not the interesting part." He opened a marked page titled *'Masūrikā Nidanam.'* "Madhavakara drew from ancient texts – *Charaka Saṃhitā, Suśruta Saṃhitā, Ashtāngahridayasaṃhitā, Ashtāṅgasaṅgraha,* and *Suddhasara.* He detailed how *Masūrikā* affected the *Vata, Pitta, and Kapha* doshas, along with its treatment."

"And these are written around the fifteenth century?" Tārā asked, her earlier frustration returning.

"Eighth century," Nana replied quietly. "And *Vagbhata's* work is from the seventh century – when smallpox was just establishing itself around the Mediterranean."

Tārā's jaw dropped. "Wait... what?"

Nana handed her another book, the second volume of an English translation of *Suśruta Saṃhitā* by Kavi Kunjlala Bhisagratna. Her fingers traced the words: '*Masūrikā* is a yellow or copper coloured pustule, attended with pain, fever, and burning, appearing all over the body, on the face, and inside the cavity of the mouth.'

"*Maharishi Suśruta* mentions it under *kshudra roga*, prescribing treatments similar to *kuṣṭha* or skin diseases. They used everything from medicated clarified butters to venesection and bloodletting for various skin diseases. *Masūrikā* is just one of many skin ailments mentioned."

"But there's more," he continued. "*Āyurveda* had a dedicated branch called *Āgada-tantra* dealing with poisons and toxins, applying specific concoctions to skin punctures."

"So that's where inoculation originated?" Tārā's eyes lit up.

"Maybe!" Nana replied cryptically.

"Hold on! Are you saying we had two different successful treatment systems? That's incredible!"

"Precisely! By the seventh century, we had extensive specialist knowledge and frameworks. Regardless of whether inoculation emerged from these techniques or developed independently - What's undeniable is that long before the fifteenth century, *Bhārat* was successfully treating smallpox – one way or another."

"So it went from India to Turkey?" Each answer seemed to trigger a cascade of revelations that left Tārā reeling, like tremors following an intellectual earthquake.

"Not just Turkey, but to the middle-east from where it went to Europe. And that should not surprise you. By the late 8th century CE, Persian physicians already held Hindu medicine in high regard. Due to this reputation, Harun al-Rashid (r. 786-809 CE) who was one of the most famous and significant Abbasid Caliphs invited an Indian physician named Mankiya to Baghdad. He requested Mankiya to bring Āyurvedic books and serve as his personal physician. Under al-Rashid's direction, these Sanskrit texts, including the fundamental works *Charaka Saṃhitā* and *Suśruta Saṃhitā* were first translated into Pahlavi and then into Arabic. So my dear, by the 8th century, Bhārat was already uplifting other ancient cultures by sharing its knowledge generously." Nana replied, plucking this gem of a story from his knowledge bank and sharing it just as effortlessly.

Their deep dive into ancient medical texts was interrupted by Urmila appearing with the cordless landline. As Nana took the call from an old friend, Tārā turned to her mother with a dramatically woeful expression.

"Āyī, I hereby renounce *masūr daal* forever!" she declared, hand placed solemnly over her heart.

Urmila raised an eyebrow. "Oh? Is this like last month's no-carb revolution? Or wait—the protein-only quest from March?" She caught herself, quickly adding, "I mean, your nutrition regime?"

Tārā shot her an icy look. Her mother knew exactly how to hit a nerve, referencing her parade of abandoned diets. It was not her fault that every new eating plan ultimately surrendered to her love affair with food. The aromas from her mother's kitchen were impossible to resist—each diet ending in an inevitable reunion with beloved dishes. And *masūr daal...* it had always held a special place in her heart, its tempting aroma often being the final straw in her dietary resolutions.

"You know what?" Urmila shook her head, "This smallpox obsession needs to end. Nana's mind is like the entire library—" she gestured expansively at the book-lined walls, "—world history, *Ramayana, Mahabharata,* the mysteries of the cosmos in Astronomy, the poetry of *Gaṇita,* the depths of *Kāśmīra Śaivdarśana,* the stories etched in temple architecture, even the forgotten meanings of our traditional tattoos... yet for ten days straight, it's been nothing but smallpox!"

Nana finished his call and handed back the cordless to Urmila.

"Nana, please," Urmila pleaded, pausing at the doorway, "tell her something wonderful. Something that does not involve pustules or infections." Her voice softened with maternal concern. "Or at least let her enjoy her *masūr daal* in peace!"

As Urmila's footsteps faded down the hallway, Nana turned to Tārā with a bewildered expression.

CHAPTER 12

MAHA BHĀRAT

· ·

"Nana, *goṣṭa sāṅga!»*

Nana's eyes crinkled with practised resistance. "You're not a little girl for stories anymore, Tārā Rānī," but his protest melted like ghee in summer. "Though perhaps age is no barrier for stories, is it? What would you like to hear?" He settled into his familiar spot beside her.

"Urmi's orders - nothing with pus or infections, remember!" Their shared laughter rippled through the room, recalling Urmila's unexpected outburst.

"Well, that puts the *Putana* story strictly off-limits,"Nana quipped.

"Oh,the flying Putana rakshasi who hunts young children, only to have Krishna drain her life force through her breast milk." Tārā's mind wandered to countless evenings where three young children would drift into dreams, carried by Nana's mesmerising voice.

Nana leaned forward, his storyteller's voice shifting to that of a teacher. "Would it have stayed with you if I had simply explained that 'pu' means pus and 'tana' means body? That our ancestors encoded medical knowledge in stories - the flying demoness representing an airborne infection, and possibly *Krishna's* triumph over it? Think deeper, Tārā Rānī," his eyes twinkled with that familiar look that preceded a revelation. "Why do you think *Krishna*, among all deities, was specifically a cowherd when he slayed *Putana*? Maybe our ancestors observed that Gau-pālaka, those who spent their lives among cows, may have been protected from the worst forms of *masurika*. The mild pustules from cowpox may have saved them from the devastating smallpox. *Krishna's* intimate connection with cows could be more than just divine play!"

"Huh... who knew!" Tārā's world tilted slightly with another revelation. "So when Edward Jenner 'discovered' vaccination using cowpox..."

"He rediscovered what our ancestors had known for millennia," Nana completed her thought.

"Let's venture somewhere else tonight," Nana suggested, his voice warming. "I've just finished re-reading the *Mahabharata*. It's still fresh in my mind."

"Is that from those precious hard-bound books you never let anyone borrow?" Tārā's question carried both curiosity and gentle teasing.

Nana's eyes softened. "Yes, the *Mahabharata* series your Ājī gave me for our 25th anniversary. She quietly saved for years to buy that set." His voice held a tender note that made Tārā's heart squeeze.

Settling deeper into his storyteller's pose, Nana's voice took on that familiar richness that had lulled three children to sleep countless times before. "Picture this: The great war had ended, and *Yudhisthara* stood amidst devastation. Mountains of charred bodies, endless funeral pyres, bones of fallen elephants and horses piled like ghostly hills. Gurus, friends, family – all sacrificed in this ravenous war fought to restore dharma." The gravity in his voice made the ancient scene come alive in the quiet bedroom.

"This brought him to an existential crisis," Nana continued, his teaching tone emerging naturally. "That's when *ŚrīKṛṣṇa* directed him to seek wisdom from his grandfather, *Bhīṣma*, the grandsire of the *Kuru* dynasty. The *Anuśāshana Parva* captures this profound conversation between grandfather and grandson – where *Bhīṣmadeva's* love and wisdom rescue *Yudhisthira's* broken spirit."

Nana's gentle pat on her shoulder punctuated his next revelation. "But here's what might surprise you,

Tārā Rānī. Within this text, *Bhīṣma* traces the lineages of revered sages – not just from the *Mahabharata* era, but reaching back to Ramayana and beyond. Such is the antiquity of this divine bhumi."

"*Maharishi Suśruta, Kasiraja, Divodas, Madhuschanda –* and their entire lineage, both ancestors and descendants – they're all acknowledged by *Bhīṣma* in this administration manual from at least 7000 years ago." Nana's words began to blur at the edges of Tārā's consciousness.

"Hmmm, *Mahabharata* is history," she murmured, sleep tugging at her awareness. "*Suśruta* was before *Mahabharata* times. He knew about *Masūrikā*…I still love eating m*asūr*. All this happened thousands of years ago…"

Nana watched over her as muttering Tārā surrendered to *Nidradevi.*

# # #

Her feet registered the unfamiliar sensation of dust between her toes. Strange fabric draped her body, and a calico bag hung across her chest like it belonged there – though she knew it did not. Everything felt both foreign and eerily familiar.

Where am I? What is this place?

Something shimmered in the distance, pulling her forward like a moth to flame.

As she approached the shimmer, reality shifted. The ground beneath her feet simply vanished. Voices filtered through her unconsciousness, and hands steadied her. Her eyes fluttered open to meet a gaze that sent her spiraling back into darkness.

The next time consciousness returned, she found herself looking into eyes that held the wisdom of universes. "If you keep fainting like this," a voice like liquid honey teased, "I will not be able to tell *Arjuna* the *Gita*. How will I instigate him to fight for what is right and defend *Dharma*?"

Recognition hit her like a thunderbolt – *ŚrīKṛṣṇa* himself! Her fingers clutched the rough fabric of the calico bag, seeking something solid in this surreal moment. "What am I doing here with this...this inoculation bag?" The words stumbled out, barely a whisper.

Arjuna's voice cut through her daze, matter-of-fact yet magnificent. "All our troops are inoculated already.

There at the edge of the battlefield is the medical camp. *Guruvarya Suśruta* and many eminent surgeons have been supervising this effort for several decades already."

"Head that way," *ŚrīKṛṣṇa* directed, pointing beyond the *Kuru* army's position. His touch on her shoulder sent divine electricity coursing through her body, raising goosebumps in its wake.

"Wake up! You've slept through the alarm Tārā!»

Reality crashed through her dream like a breaking wave. The alarm had been screaming unheard, and her mother's voice yanked her back to the present. "*Āyī*, I was about to listen to *Bhagavad Gītā* from *Krishna* himself!" Beyond frustrated - she was almost angry. "Why did you have to wake me up just then? Now I'll never know what other advice he could have given me!"

Urmila's calm response annoyed her further "That's okay, let me fill you in. He said you have absolute control over taking action and doing your duty, but no control or claim over the results. So stop procrastinating and hit the gym. Just do it, Tārā." Her mother's plea carried echoes of divine instruction.

Tārā leaped from her bed, embracing her mother before charging out with raised fist, "YES, I actually can do something about this!"

That evening found Tārā in an unexpected place. She lit the agarbattī and waited for Nana to begin the *parvācā.* As he began the *Vishnu sahasranama,* she followed along. Nana slowed his pace for her unpracticed chanting to catch up. The *shlokas* became a bridge between generations.

After the final verses faded, Tārā did something unprecedented. She placed her laptop before the *devghar,* its screen facing the *murtis.* Baffled, Nana asked her, "What are you doing?"

"I've been thinking, Nana," she began, her voice carrying newfound purpose. "Why did any of my research not give me the *dṛṣṭikoṇa* that you showed me? Why was this knowledge hidden from me until now? Why were our native contributions sidelined when they were clearly extraordinary?" She paused, conviction building in her voice. "I realised I have two choices – fret over what's wrong or do something about it. I choose action."

Her eyes sparkled with determination. "I have decided to right this wrong. I'm starting a blog, showing it to *Gaṇapati* first. I'm going to share what I've learned, so another Tārā does not make the same bet I did." Her triumphant declaration ended with a playful wink.

A smile bloomed across Nana's face as Tārā bent to touch his feet, seeking blessings. His *"yashsawi bhava"* resonated through her being, not just as words but as a calling.

This was not an ending. This was a beginning.

GLOSSARY

Āyī (आई): Mother

Āgada-tantra (आगद तंत्र): Branch of Āyurveda focusing on toxicology

Agarbattī (अगरबत्ती): Incense sticks

Ājī (आजी): Grandmother

Ākāśakandīl (आकाशकंदील): Traditional lantern used during Diwali

Akkhā Masūr (अख्खा मसूर): Whole red lentils

Amṛta Kalaśa (अमृत कलश): Divine pot of immortality nectar

Anuśāshana Parva (अनुशासन पर्व): Section of Mahabharata dealing with instruction

Ashtāngahridayasaṃhitā (अष्टांग हृदय): Classical Āyurvedic text

Ashtāṅgasaṅgraha (अष्टांग संग्रह): Comprehensive Āyurvedic compilation

Ātyā (आत्या): Paternal aunt

Āyurveda Tīrtha (आयुर्वेद तीर्थ): Super specialist practitioner of Āyurveda

Basantaroga (बसंतरोग): Spring disease also known as Vasanta roga (वसन्त रोग)

Bhagavad Gītā (भगवद्गीता): Sacred Hindu text, dialogue between Krishna and Arjuna

Bhagavān Dhanvantari (भगवान धन्वंतरि): Hindu god of medicine and healing

Bhārat (भारत): Traditional/native name for India

Bhārat Sarkār (भारत सरकार): Indian government

Bhīṣma (भीष्म): Great warrior and philosopher in Mahabharata

Bhuvaneśvarī (भुवनेश्वरी): Goddess of the Universe

Chaha (चहा): Tea

Charaka Saṃhitā (चरक संहिता): Foundational text of Āyurveda

Cowries (कौड़ी): Small shells once used as currency, now used in rituals

Dahī (दही): Yogurt/curd

Devghar (देवघर): Home shrine; sacred space for worship in Hindu homes

Devatās (देवता): Deities

Devī/Devīs (देवी): Goddess

Dhābbā (ढाबा): Located along highways, these are inexpensive Indian restaurant that serves Punjabi food.

Dharma (धर्म): Moral and cosmic order

Dṛṣṭikoṇa (दृष्टिकोन): Perspective/viewpoint

Pharāḷ (फराळ): Traditional Marathi Diwali snacks

Gaṇapati (गणपती): Another name for Lord Ganesha

Gaṅgājala (गंगाजल): Holy water from River Ganges

Gaṇita (गणित): Traditional Indian mathematics

Garam (गरम): Hot

Garam Garam Bhākrī (गरम गरम भाकरी): Hot millet/jowar flatbread

Gau-palak (गौपालक): Cowherd

Goṣṭa sāṅga (गोष्ट सांग): "Tell me a story"

Guḷa (गुळ): Jaggery; unrefined cane sugar

Gallī (गल्ली): Street; narrow lane

Iḍlī-Sāmbhār (इडली सांभर): South Indian breakfast dish combining rice cakes with lentil soup

Inoculation: Early form of vaccination

Jāmbūla (जांभूळ): Java plum; Indian blackberry

Janeū (जनेऊ): Sacred thread worn by initiated Hindu males

Jāū de (जाऊ दे): Marathi phrase meaning "let it go/ let it be"

Kāśmīra Śaivdarśana (काश्मीर शैवदर्शन): School of Hindu philosophy

Khamaṅga kākaḍī (खमंग काकडी): Spiced cucumber salad

Kuṣṭha (कुष्ठ): Category of skin diseases in Āyurveda

Kuṭhe āhe te Vaccine (कुठे आहे ते व्हॅक्सीन): Where is the vaccine?

Laxmi (लक्ष्मी): Goddess of wealth and prosperity

Mādhavācārya (माधवाचार्य): Ancient Indian physician

Merā Bhārat Mahān (मेरा भारत महान): My India is Great

Mul-mul (मलमल): Fine cotton cloth

Nāḍī (नाडी): Pulse; energy channel

Nana (नाना): Grandfather; paternal grandfather

Nārāyaṇī (नारायणी): Another name for Goddess Lakshmi

Neem (नीम): Medicinal tree

Paramparā (परंपरा): Tradition; lineage

Pārtha (पार्थ): Another name of Arjuna

Parvācā (पर्वाचा): Evening prayers; evening worship time

Peśvā (पेशवा): Prime minister of Maratha empire

Pracaṇḍa (प्रचंड): Intense; fierce

Pradhāna (प्रधान): Chief; principal

Roga (रोग): Disease

Sābūdāṇā (साबूदाणा): Sago pearls

Sābūdāṇā Khicaḍī (साबूदाणा खिचडी): Dish made with sago pearls

Samaī (समई): Traditional brass oil lamp used in worship

Saṅkramaṇa (संक्रमण): Infection/transmission

Satyam ca svādhyāya pravacane ca (सत्यम् च स्वाध्याय प्रवचने च): Truth should be learned and taught

Śītalā (शीतला): One who is gentle and cool.

Śītalā Mata (शीतला माता): Mother Śītalā - Goddess associated with smallpox

Suśruta Saṃhitā (सुश्रुत संहिता): Ancient Sanskrit text on medicine and surgery

Surya Gayatri (सूर्य गायत्री): Sacred Sanskrit verse dedicated to Sun God

Tāk (ताक): Buttermilk

Tapasya (तपस्या): Dedicated effort; spiritual discipline

Tārā Rānī (तारा राणी): Queen Tārā

Tikhat (तिखट): Spicy

Upanishad (उपनिषद्): Ancient Sanskrit texts on Hindu philosophy

Vaidya (वैद्य): Traditional physician

Vata (वात): One of three doshas in Āyurveda

Vishnu Sahasranama (विष्णु सहस्रनाम): Thousand names of Bhagwan Vishnu

Wada (वाडा): Traditional Maharashtrian mansion

SANSKRIT SHLOKAS APPEARING IN THIS BOOK

$\mathbf{T}$he Sūrya Gāyatrī: A Sacred Invocation to the Solar Principle

The Sūrya Gāyatrī Mantra stands as one of the most significant Sanskrit verses in the Vedic tradition, dedicated to invoking the divine solar energy. This sacred mantra is traditionally recited for physical vitality, mental clarity, and spiritual enlightenment.

Sanskrit Text:

ॐ भास्कराय विद्महे
महातेजाय धीमहि
तन्न: सूर्य: प्रचोदयात्

Transliteration:

> oṃ bhāskarāya vidmahe
>
> mahātejāya dhīmahi
>
> tannaḥ sūryaḥ pracodayāt

Word-by-Word Analysis:

- oṃ (ॐ): The primordial sound, representing universal consciousness

- bhāskarāya (भास्कराय): To the Light-maker

- vidmahe (विद्महे): We know or perceive

- mahātejāya (महातेजाय): To the greatly radiant one

- dhīmahi (धीमहि): We meditate upon

- tannaḥ (तन्नः): That (for) us

- sūryaḥ (सूर्यः): The Sun

- pracodayāt (प्रचोदयात्): May illuminate/inspire

Meaning:

"We meditate upon the radiant light-maker (Sun); we contemplate the magnificent effulgence. May that divine Sun illuminate our intellect."

This mantra is traditionally chanted during morning prayers, particularly during the practice of Sūrya Namaskāra, as a means to connect with and harness solar energy for physical, mental, and spiritual well-being.

The Samarpana Shloka: A Verse of Complete Surrender

This profound Sanskrit verse, found in both the Mukundamala and Srimad Bhagavatam (with slight variations), embodies the essence of complete surrender (samarpana) to the Divine. It represents the ultimate expression of karma yoga, where all actions are offered to the Supreme.

Sanskrit Text:

कायेन वाचा मनसेन्द्रियैर्वा

बुद्ध्यात्मना वा प्रकृतिस्वभावात्

करोमि यद्यत्सकलं परस्मै

नारायणायेति समर्पयामि

Transliteration:

kāyena vācā manasendriyairvā

buddhyātmanā vā prakṛtisvabhāvāt

karomi yadyat sakalaṃ parasmai

nārāyaṇāyeti samarpayāmi

Word-by-Word Analysis:

- kāyena (कायेन): By the body
- vācā (वाचा): By speech
- manasā (मनसा): By the mind
- indriyaiḥ (इन्द्रियैः): By the senses

- vā (वा): Or
- buddhyā (बुद्ध्या): By intellect
- ātmanā (आत्मना): By the self
- prakṛti-svabhāvāt (प्रकृतिस्वभावात्): Due to natural tendencies
- karomi (करोमि): I do
- yadyat (यद्यत्): Whatever
- sakalam (सकलं): All
- parasmai (परस्मै): To the Supreme
- nārāyaṇāya (नारायणाय): To Narayana
- iti (इति): Thus
- samarpayāmi (समर्पयामि): I surrender/offer

Meaning:

"Whatever I perform with my body, speech, mind, or senses,

Through intellect, self, or natural tendencies,

All these actions, whatever they may be,

I surrender completely to Lord Narayana."

The Śītalāṣṭakam: Eight Verses in Praise of Goddess Śītalā

First, the Viniyoga (Application):

Sanskrit:

अस्य श्रीशीतलास्तोत्रस्य महादेव ऋषिः ।

अनुष्टुप् छन्दः । शीतला देवता ।

लक्ष्मीर्बीजम् । भवानी शक्तिः ।

सर्वविस्फोटकनिवृत्यर्थे जपे विनियोगः ॥

Transliteration:

asya śrīśītalāstotrasya mahādeva ṛṣiḥ |

anuṣṭup chandaḥ | śītalā devatā |

lakṣmīrbījam | bhavānī śaktiḥ |

sarvavisphōṭakanivṛtyarthe jape viniyogaḥ ||

Meaning:

Of this Śītalā Stotra, Mahadeva is the Rishi (seer),

Anushtup is the meter, Śītalā is the deity,

Lakshmi is the seed, Bhavani is the power,

The application is for the prevention of all eruptions through recitation.

1.

Sanskrit:

ईश्वर उवाच ।

वन्देऽहं शीतलां देवीं रासभस्थां दिगम्बराम् ।

मार्जनीकलशोपेतां शूर्पालङ्कृतमस्तकाम् ॥

Transliteration:

īśvara uvāca |

vande'haṃ śītalāṃ devīṃ rāsabhasthāṃ digambarām |

mārjanīkalaśopetāṃ śūrpālaṅkṛtamastakām ||

Meaning:

Ishvara said:

I bow to Goddess Śītalā, who rides upon a donkey, is sky-clad (unclothed),

Holds a broom and water pot, and whose head is adorned with a winnowing fan.

2.

Sanskrit:

वन्देऽहं शीतलां देवीं सर्वरोगभयापहाम् ।

यामासाद्य निवर्तेत विस्फोटकभयं महत् ॥

Transliteration:

vande'haṃ śītalāṃ devīṃ sarvarogabhayāpahām |

yāmāsādya nivarteta visphoṭakabhayaṃ mahat | |

Meaning:

I bow to Goddess Śītalā, who removes the fear of all diseases,

By whose grace the great fear of eruptions (smallpox) is dispelled.

3.

Sanskrit:

शीतले शीतले चेति यो ब्रूयद्दाहपीडितः ।

विस्फोटकभयं घोरं क्षिप्रं तस्य प्रणश्यति ॥

Transliteration:

śītale śītale ceti yo brūyaddāhapīḍitaḥ |

visphoṭakabhayaṃ ghoraṃ kṣipraṃ tasya praṇaśyati | |

Meaning:

One who, afflicted with burning fever, calls out "Shitale, Shitale,"

Their terrible fear of eruptions quickly vanishes.

4.

Sanskrit:

यस्त्वामुदकमध्ये तु ध्यात्वा सम्पूजयेन्नरः ।
विस्फोटकभयं घोरं गृहे तस्य न जायते ॥

Transliteration:

yastvāmudakamadhye tu dhyātvā sampūjayennaraḥ |

visphoṭakabhayaṃ ghoraṃ gṛhe tasya na jāyate ||

Meaning:

One who meditates upon and worships you in water,

The terrible fear of eruptions never enters their home.

5.

Sanskrit:

शीतले ज्वरदग्धस्य पूतिगन्धयुतस्य च ।
प्रणष्टचक्षुषः पुंसस्त्वामाहुर्जीवनौषधम् ॥

Transliteration:

śītale jvaradagdhasya pūtigandhayutasya ca |

praṇaṣṭacakṣuṣaḥ puṃsastvāmāhurjīvanauṣadham ||

Meaning:

O Śītalā, for one burnt with fever and afflicted with putrid conditions,

And for those with lost vision, you are called the life-giving medicine.

6.

Sanskrit:

शीतले तनुजान् रोगान् नृणां हरसि दुस्त्यजान् ।
विस्फोटकविदीर्णानां त्वमेकाऽमृतवर्षिणी ॥

Transliteration:

śītale tanujān rogān nṛṇāṃ harasi dustyajān |

visphoṭakavidīrṇānāṃ tvamekā'mṛtavarṣiṇī ||

Meaning:

O Śītalā, you remove the stubborn bodily diseases of humans;

For those afflicted with eruptions, you alone shower nectar.

7.

Sanskrit:

गलगण्डग्रहा रोगा ये चान्ये दारुणा नृणाम् ।
त्वदनुध्यानमात्रेण शीतले यान्ति सङ्क्षयम् ॥

Transliteration:

galagaṇḍagrahā rogā ye cānye dāruṇā nṛṇām |

tvadanudhyānamātreṇa śītale yānti saṅkṣayam ||

Meaning:

Diseases like goiter and other terrible afflictions of humans,

O Śītalā, merely by meditating on you, they are destroyed.

8.

Sanskrit:

न मन्त्रो नौषधं तस्य पापरोगस्य विद्यते ।

त्वामेकां शीतले धात्रीं नान्यां पश्यामि देवताम् ॥

Transliteration:

na mantro nauṣadhaṃ tasya pāparogasya vidyate |

tvāmekāṃ śītale dhātrīṃ nānyāṃ paśyāmi devatām ||

Meaning:

There exists no mantra or medicine for that sinful disease;

O Śītalā, I see you alone as the sustaining goddess, no other deity.

9.

Sanskrit:

मृणालतन्तुसदृशीं नाभिहृन्मध्यसंस्थिताम् ।

यस्त्वां सञ्चिन्तयेद्देवि तस्य मृत्युर्न जायते ॥

Transliteration:

mṛṇālatantusadṛśīṃ nābihṛnmadhyasaṃsthitām |

yastvāṃ sañcintayeddevi tasya mṛtyurna jāyate ||

Meaning:

Like a lotus fiber, residing in the heart-center of the navel,

O Goddess, whoever meditates upon you thus, death does not come to them.

10.

Sanskrit:

अष्टकं शीतलादेव्या यो नरः प्रपठेत्सदा ।

विस्फोटकभयं घोरं गृहे तस्य न जायते ॥

Transliteration:

aṣṭakaṃ śītalādevyā yo naraḥ prapaṭhetsadā |

visphoṭakabhayaṃ ghoraṃ gṛhe tasya na jāyate ||

Meaning:

The person who regularly recites these eight verses of Goddess Śītalā,

The terrible fear of eruptions never enters their home.

11.

Sanskrit:

श्रोतव्यं पठितव्यं च श्रद्धाभक्तिसमन्वितैः ।

उपसर्गविनाशाय परं स्वस्त्ययनं महत् ॥

Transliteration:

śrotavyaṃ paṭhitavyaṃ ca
śraddhābhāktisamanvitaiḥ |

upasargavināśāya paraṃ svastyayanaṃ mahat ||

Meaning:

This should be heard and recited with faith and devotion;

It is the supreme blessing for the destruction of epidemics.

12.

Sanskrit:

शीतले त्वं जगन्माता शीतले त्वं जगत्पिता ।

शीतले त्वं जगद्धात्री शीतलायै नमो नमः ॥

Transliteration:

śītale tvaṃ jaganmātā śītale tvaṃ jagatpitā |

śītale tvaṃ jagaddhātrī śītalāyai namo namaḥ ||

Meaning:

O Śītalā, you are the mother of the universe, you are the father of the universe,

O Śītalā, you are the sustainer of the universe, repeated salutations to Śītalā.

13.

Sanskrit:

रासभो गर्दभश्चैव खरो वैशाखनन्दनः ।

शीतलावाहनश्चैव दूर्वाकन्दनिकृन्तनः ॥

Transliteration:

rāsabho gardabhaścaiva kharo vaiśākhanandanaḥ |

śītalāvāhanaścaiva dūrvākandanikṛntanaḥ ||

Meaning:

The donkey (called by various names - Rasabha, Gardabha, Khara, Vaishakhanandana),

Is Śītalā's vehicle and the cutter of Durva grass roots.

14.

Sanskrit:

एतानि खरनामानि शीतलाग्रे तु यः पठेत् ।

तस्य गेहे शिशूनां च शीतलारुङ् न जायते ॥

Transliteration:

etāni kharanāmāni śītalāgre tu yaḥ paṭhet |

tasya gehe śiśūnāṃ ca śītalāruṅ na jāyate ||

Meaning:

Whoever recites these names of the donkey before Śītalā,

In their home, children will not be afflicted by Śītalā's disease.

15.

Sanskrit:

शीतलाष्टकमेवेदं न देयं यस्यकस्यचित् ।

दातव्यं च सदा तस्मै श्रद्धाभक्तियुताय वै ॥

Transliteration:

śītalāṣṭakamevedaṃ na deyaṃ yasyakasyacit |

dātavyaṃ ca sadā tasmai śraddhābhaktiyutāya vai ||

Meaning:

This Śītalāshtak should not be given to just anyone;

It should be given only to those who possess faith and devotion.

Final Colophon:

॥ इति श्रीस्कन्दपुराणे शीतलाष्टकं सम्पूर्णम् ॥

Transliteration:

|| iti śrīskandapurāṇe śītalāṣṭakaṃ sampūrṇam ||

Meaning:

Thus ends the Śītalāshtak from the Sri Skanda Purana.

NOTES

R ani Tarabai (1675-1761) was a formidable Maratha
queen who played a crucial role in preserving
and expanding the Maratha Empire during a critical
period of its history. Born to Hambir Rao Mohite, the
commander-in-chief of Chhatrapati Shivaji's army,
Tarabai was well-trained in military strategy, diplomacy,
and statecraft from a young age. After the death of her
husband, Chhatrapati Rajaram, in 1700, she assumed the
role of regent for her young son and led the Maratha
resistance against the Mughal Empire. Despite facing
a massive Mughal army led by Emperor Aurangzeb,
Tarabai's exceptional leadership skills, military acumen,
and strategic brilliance allowed the Marathas to not only
survive but thrive. She personally led armies into battle,
forged crucial alliances, and implemented innovative
guerrilla warfare tactics that kept the Mughals at bay. Her
seven-year regency was marked by significant territorial

expansion and the strengthening of Maratha power, laying the foundation for the empire's future dominance in the Indian subcontinent.

REFERENCES

Introduction:

1.   Holwell, J. Z. (John Zephaniah). *An Account of the Manner of Inoculating for the Small Pox in the East IndiesWith Some Observations on the Practice and Mode of Treating That Disease in Those Parts*, 2016. https://www.gutenberg.org/ebooks/52722.

2.   Jenner, Edward. *Instructions for Vaccine Inoculation.* London : D.N. Shury, 1801. http://archive.org/details/b22010440.

3.   ———. *Letters of Edward Jenner, and Other Documents Concerning the Early History of Vaccination.* Baltimore : Johns Hopkins University Press, 1983. http://archive.org/details/lettersofedwardj0000jenn.

4.   ———. *On the Varieties and Modifications of the Vaccine Pustule, Occasioned by an Herpetic State of the Skin.*

Cheltenham : H. Ruff, 1806. http://archive.org/details/b2200953x.

5. ———. *The Origin of the Vaccine Inoculation : Jenner, Edward, 1749-1823. n 79086454 : Free Download, Borrow, and Streaming*. D.N Shury, 1801. https://archive.org/details/b22010452.

6. Kochhar, Rajesh. 'Smallpox in the Modern Scientific and Colonial Contexts 1721–1840'. *Journal of Biosciences* 36, no. 5 (1 December 2011): 761–68. https://doi.org/10.1007/s12038-011-9146-6.

7. Lahariya, Chandrakant. 'A Brief History of Vaccines & Vaccination in India'. *The Indian Journal of Medical Research* 139, no. 4 (April 2014): 491–511. https://www.ncbi.nlm.nih.gov/pmc/articles/PMC4078488/.

8. Boylston, Arthur. 'The Origins of Vaccination: No Inoculation, No Vaccination'. *Journal of the Royal Society of Medicine* 106, no. 10 (2013): 395–98. https://doi.org/10.1177/0141076813499293.

9. Brink, Susan. 'What's The Real Story About The Milkmaid And The Smallpox Vaccine?' *NPR*, 1 February 2018, sec. Health. https://www.npr.org/sections/goatsandsoda/2018/02/01/582370199/whats-the-real-story-about-the-milkmaid-and-the-smallpox-vaccine.

10. Office for Science and Society. 'The White Lie at the Heart of Vaccine History'. https://www.mcgill.ca/oss/article/medical-critical-thinking-history/white-lie-heart-vaccine-history.

11. Science History Institute. 'Louis Pasteur'. https://www.sciencehistory.org/education/scientific-biographies/louis-pasteur/.

12. Dharampal. Indian Science and Technology in the Eighteenth Century: Some Contemporary European Accounts. Delhi: Impex India, 1971.

13. Apffel-Marglin, Frederique. "Smallpox in Two Systems of Knowledge", WIDER Working Papers (1986-2000) 1987/017 Helsinki: UNU-WIDER, 1987.

Chapter 1: Suitcases and Stillness

1. Serra Selek and Matheus Marques. 'An Overview of the Mental Health Crisis with COVID-19 in India'. Harvard University, 31 July 2021. https://projects.iq.harvard.edu/aia/news/overview-mental-health-crisis-covid-19-india.

2. Runwal, Priyanka. 'How India's COVID-19 Crisis Became the Worst in the World', 9 May 2021. https://www.sciencenews.org/article/coronavirus-covid-india-crisis-social-distancing-masks-variant.

3. Gordon, Stewart. "Responses to Family Invasion (1680–1719)." Chapter. In The Marathas 1600–1818, 91–113. The New Cambridge History of India. Cambridge: Cambridge University Press, 1993.

4. Eaton, Richard M. "Tarabai (1675–1761): The Rise of Brahmins in Politics." Chapter. In A Social History of the Deccan, 1300–1761: Eight Indian Lives, 177–202. The New Cambridge History of India. Cambridge: Cambridge University Press, 2005.

Chapter 2: Morning tea stirs a memory

1. CDC. 'Clinical Signs and Symptoms of Smallpox'. Smallpox, 6 November 2024. https://www.cdc.gov/smallpox/hcp/clinical-signs/index.html.

2. World Health Organisation. 'Smallpox'. Health. https://www.who.int/health-topics/smallpox.

Chapter 3: Netopedia Triumphs

1. The Jenner Institute. 'About Edward Jenner'. Web Page. https://www.jenner.ac.uk/about/edward-jenner.

2. Baxby, D. 'Edward Jenner's Inquiry; a Bicentenary Analysis'. *Vaccine* 17, no. 4 (28 January 1999): 301–7. https://doi.org/10.1016/s0264-410x(98)00207-2.

3. Belongia, Edward A., and Allison L. Naleway. 'Smallpox Vaccine: The Good, the Bad, and the Ugly'. *Clinical*

Medicine and Research 1, no. 2 (April 2003): 87–92. https://www.ncbi.nlm.nih.gov/pmc/articles/PMC1069029/.

4. 'Edward Jenner'. In *Wikipedia*, 25 November 2024. https://en.wikipedia.org/w/index.php?title=Edward_Jenner&oldid=1259544923.

5. Gross, C. P., and K. A. Sepkowitz. 'The Myth of the Medical Breakthrough: Smallpox, Vaccination, and Jenner Reconsidered'. *International Journal of Infectious Diseases: IJID: Official Publication of the International Society for Infectious Diseases* 3, no. 1 (1998): 54–60. https://doi.org/10.1016/s1201-9712(98)90096-0.

6. Riedel, Stefan. 'Edward Jenner and the History of Smallpox and Vaccination'. *Proceedings (Baylor University. Medical Center)* 18, no. 1 (January 2005): 21–25. https://www.ncbi.nlm.nih.gov/pmc/articles/PMC1200696/.

Chapter 4: Postcards from the Past

1. Brilliant, Lawrence B.. The Management of Smallpox Eradication in India. United States: University of Michigan Press, 1985.

2. Bhattacharya, Sanjoy, and Carlos Eduardo D'Avila Pereira Campani. 'Re-Assessing the Foundations: Worldwide Smallpox Eradication, 1957–67'. *Medical History* 64, no. 1 (January 2020): 71–93. https://doi.org/10.1017/mdh.2019.77.

3. 'Smallpox Eradication in India, 1972-1977 | India Engages the Pandemic · Online Exhibits'. https://apps.lib.umich.edu/online-exhibits/exhibits/show/smallpox-eradication-india/indian-engages-pandemic.

4. Gelfand, H M. 'A Critical Examination of the Indian Smallpox Eradication Program.' *American Journal of Public Health and the Nations Health* 56, no. 10 (October 1966): 1634–51. https://www.ncbi.nlm.nih.gov/pmc/articles/PMC1257297/.

Chapter 5: The Divine Deliverance

1. Ferrari, Fabrizio. 'Old Rituals for New Threats. The Post-Smallpox Career of Śītalā, the Cold Mother of Bengal.' *Ritual Matters. Dynamic Dimensions in Practice, Edited by C. BROSIUS and U. HÜSKEN (New Delhi: Routledge)*, 1 January 2010. https://www.academia.edu/1633917/Old_rituals_for_new_threats_The_post_smallpox_career_of_%C5%9A%C4%ABtal%C4%81_the_cold_mother_of_Bengal.

2. Ralph, Nicloas. *The Goddess Śītalā And Epidemic Smallpox In Bengal , Author(s): Ralph W. Nicholas Source: The Journal of Asian Studies, Vol. 41, No. 1 (Nov., 1981), Pp. 21-44 Published by: Association for Asian Studies.* http://archive.org/details/thegoddesssitalaandepidemicsmallpoxinbengal.

3. 'Shitala'. In *Wikipedia*, 7 November 2024. https://en.wikipedia.org/w/index.php?title=Shitala&oldid=1255913865.

Chapter 6: Conquest through Contagion

1. Errico, Peter d'. 'Jeffery Amherst and Smallpox Blankets', n.d. https://people.umass.edu/derrico/amherst/lord_jeff.html.

2. ASM.org. 'Investigating the Smallpox Blanket Controversy'. https://asm.org:443/Articles/2023/November/Investigating-the-Smallpox-Blanket-Controversy.

3. 'Native American Disease and Epidemics'. In *Wikipedia*, 2 December 2024. https://en.wikipedia.org/w/index.php?title=Native_American_disease_and_epidemics&oldid=1260834475.

4. Patterson, Kristine B., and Thomas Runge. "Smallpox and the Native American." *The American Journal of the Medical Sciences* 323, no. 4 (April 1, 2002): 216–22. https://doi.org/10.1097/00000441-200204000-00009.

5. Aboriginal Heritage Office. 'A Brief Aboriginal History'. https://www.aboriginalheritage.org/history/history/.

6. Britannica Kids. 'Indigenous and European Contact in Australia'. https://kids.britannica.com/students/article/Indigenous-and-European-Contact-in-Australia/631556.

Chapter 7: Holwell's Eastern Account &
Chapter 8: Brindavan-Benaras Brahmins

1. Boylston, Arthur. 'The Origins of Inoculation'. *Journal of the Royal Society of Medicine* 105, no. 7 (July 2012): 309–13. https://doi.org/10.1258/jrsm.2012.12k044.

2. Holwell, J. Z. (John Zephaniah). 'An Account of the Manner of Inoculating for the Small Pox in the East Indies With Some Observations on the Practice and Mode of Treating That Disease in Those Parts'.

3. https://www.gutenberg.org/cache/epub/52722/pg52722-images.html.

4. 'John Zephaniah Holwell'. In *Wikipedia*, 23 November 2024. https://en.wikipedia.org/w/index.php?title=John_Zephaniah_Holwell&oldid=1259121806.

5. Reingold, Arthur. 'Smallpox—The Death of a Disease: The Inside Story of Eradicating a Worldwide Killer'. *American Journal of Epidemiology* 171, no. 3 (1 February 2010): 384–85. https://doi.org/10.1093/aje/kwp431.

Chapter 9: From Inoculation to Vaccination & Chapter 10: Digested Discoveries

1. Antoinette Emch-Deriaz [University of Florida]. 'Inoculation'. *Encyclopedia of Diderot & d'Alembert - Collaborative Translation Project*, 20 September 2016. http://hdl.handle.net/2027/spo.did2222.0000.954.

2. 'Charles-Pierre Chais'. In *Wikipedia*, 18 October 2024. https://en.wikipedia.org/w/index.php?title=Charles-Pierre_Chais&oldid=1251805776.

3. Gupta, Kshama & Mamidi, Prasad. (2023). Novel Insights into the Concepts of Masurika in Madhava Nidana. Journal

of Integrated Health Science. 10. 102-110. 10.4103/jihs. jihs_15_22.

4. Kirkpatrick, James. The Analysis of Inoculation: Comprizing the History, Theory and Practice of it .... United Kingdom: J. Buckland ... and R. Griffiths, 1761.

5. Kochhar, Rajesh. 'Smallpox in the Modern Scientific and Colonial Contexts 1721–1840'. *Journal of Biosciences* 36, no. 5 (1 December 2011): 761–68. https://doi.org/10.1007/ s12038-011-9146-6.

6. 'Madhava-Kara'. In *Wikipedia*, 30 November 2024. https://en.wikipedia.org/w/index.php?title=Madhava-kara&oldid=1260351141.

7. MD(Ayu), Dr J. V. Hebbar. 'Madhava Nidana Chapter 54 Masurika Nidanam'. Easy Ayurveda Hospital, 15 April 2023. https://www.easyayurveda.com/2023/04/15/ madhava-masurika-nidanam/.

8. 'Maitland C 1722 Account of Inoculating the Small Pox (London: J Downing)', n.d.

9. 'Vagbhata'. In *Wikipedia*, 11 October 2024. https:// en.wikipedia.org/w/index.php?title=Vagbhata&old id=1250695222.

Chapter 11: From India to Italy via Istanbul

1. 'Indian Influence on Islamic Science'. In *Wikipedia*, 13 October 2024. https://en.wikipedia.org/w/

index.php?title=Indian_influence_on_Islamic_science&oldid=1250918572.

2. 'Translation of Indian Texts into Arabic under the Abbasids – Purple Motes', 4 March 2012. https://www.purplemotes.net/2012/03/04/translation-of-indian-texts-into-arabic-under-the-abbasids/.

3. ULLMANN, MANFRED. *Islamic Medicine*. Edinburgh University Press, 1978. http://www.jstor.org/stable/10.3366/j.ctvxcrv7d.

4. Vedam, Raj, Tabassum A. Pansare, and Jagat Narula. 'Contributions of Ancient Indian Knowledge to Modern Medicine and Cardiology'. *Indian Heart Journal* 73, no. 5 (2021): 531–34. https://doi.org/10.1016/j.ihj.2021.09.010.

Chapter 12: Maha Bhārat

1. Oak, Nilesh Nilkanth. When Did The Mahabharata War Happen? The Mystery of Arundhati. United States: Amazon Digital Services LLC - Kdp, 2011.

2. Desai, Mitra. 'Sushruta and His Samhita - Part 9 - Sushruta Graced Bharat at Least 5561 BCE!' Tejomaya Bharat - Dazzling India!, 6 May 2023. https://www.tejomayabharat.com/sushruta-and-his-samhita-part-9-sushruta-graced-bharat-at-least-5561-bce/.

ACKNOWLEDGEMENTS

A book is never truly the work of a single individual. Each conversation, an insight, a moment of inspiration—contributes to a narrative larger than any one perspective. What appears as my name on the cover is, in reality, a convergence of multiple intellects, experiences, and wisdom traditions.

The selection of my book Shitala: How India enabled vaccination for the inaugural Tejas Book Competition was a momentous occasion. Attending both the Dharma in Digital Age conference and the Scholars Retreat in Atlanta in July 2024 were an enriching experience. People who had inspired me on this Indic journey - I heard them in person, and in some cases even had the opportunity to sit at their feet and learn. The mentors I met with and the friendships I made, continue to guide me even today.

Acknowledgements

Engaging with the young and curious minds from America helped me understand the profound impact my work has had. This experience was made possible by the Dharma Civilization Foundation (DCF), and I extend my heartfelt thanks to the DCF team particularly Shrikant Palkar ji and Dipti Thuse for providing this incredible opportunity to connect with energetic minds exploring their connection to the Indic ethos.

I am grateful to Dr Ajay Houde for his thoughtful gesture of taking me to the Centre for Disease Control during my Atlanta trip, as a surprise. It was an incredible experience to find Śītalā devi's murti displayed at the CDC.

I would like to thank Dr Swati Gaur for a stimulating conversation around vaccination and the historical erasure. These experiences underscore the timeless connection between faith, science, and our quest for healing.

I am also grateful to Dr Gauri Mahulikar and Shivprasad Mantri sir for their enthralling stories. From them, I learnt how to make the complex, digestible and relatable.

My dear friend Hrishikesh Kapre is the one who sent me down this rabbit-hole, for which I am thankful. He took it upon himself to translate the original Shitala book into Marathi. In the process, I was compelled to revisit parts of the story and make additions, which in turn has led to this new book being born.

Many thanks also to the prolific author Satyen Velankar for helping me locate sources at lightning speed!

I am eternally grateful to Vaidya Dr Madhuri Patil. Over the years she has been the Encyclopedia of Ayurveda for me. Where I could easily be drowning in this vast ocean of information, she gives me the exact list of sources I need to go to, where I can dive deep to get the pearls of wisdom from.

I am also grateful for the constant guidance, support and encouragement from amazing scholar-healers like Vaidya Pareexit Shevde, Vaidya Abhijeet Saraf and Dr Mala Kapadia.

I extend my gratitude to author and original researcher Nilesh Oak ji for his invaluable insights and time. He devoted precious time despite his travel schedule, to guide and help me see things in a different light.

I would like to thank my dear friend, author and an amazing storyteller Deepali Patwadkar. Her deep knowledge of Hindu traditions and customs, as well as her passion for celebrating Bharat's rich culture, have been constants in my journey. She has been my sounding board, offering thoughtful critiques and invaluable perspectives that have strengthened every chapter of this book. Thank you, Deepali, for being my pillar of strength and inspiration.

I would also like to thank Dr Anand Ranganathan for making time through his incredibly busy schedule to provide such a brilliant foreword.

You would not be reading this book, were you not drawn in by the cover. Many thanks to ace designer Horia Sidiqi for the stunning cover design!

I also want to acknowledge my dear friend and artist Falguni Gokhale, whose design for the first book inspired this redesign.

And finally, to the silent architects of this book, my family. You all know who you are and how grateful I am to have your support!

Aai, Baba, Umā-aai, Śarmelā kākī—your āshirwāds are the foundations this work is built on.

To my beautiful nephews Rudra, Kārthikēya, and niece Ēśwarī—this work is your inheritance. May you always remain curious, always question the status quo and seek the truth.

To Ēra, Bipin, Hrishikēśa and Shāraṅga—my anchors, my inspiration—without your unwavering support, this journey would have been impossible.

ABOUT THE AUTHOR

Mitra Desai is a multifaceted individual who excels as an author, entrepreneur, researcher, and speaker. Her passion for uncovering India's forgotten voices and contributions is evident in her bestselling books, "Śītalā" and "The Flag of Ananta: In Sugriva's Footsteps," both of which blend deep research with engaging fiction.

Beyond her literary achievements, Mitra Desai is also known for her extensive work in creating educational content. She has collaborated with notable figures in the Indic fields to create relevant content.

Mitra Desai's professional and personal life are marked by a cross-continental presence, with ties to both India and Australia. Her work reflects a unique ability to bridge cultures, making her a sought-after speaker and storyteller who uses a variety of mediums to convey profound messages.

At heart, Mitra Desai is a storyteller committed to sharing the depth and richness of India's heritage with a global audience.

Connect with Mitra at www.mitradesai.com and read more such fascinating stories at www.tejomayabharat.com